MACMILLAN MODERN DRAMATISTS

DIRECTORS' THEATRE

David Bradby and David Williams

MACMILLAN

First published 1988

Published by
Higher and Further Education Division
MACMILLAN PUBLISHERS LTD
Houndmills, Basingstoke, Hampshire RG21 2XS
and London
Companies and representatives
throughout the world

Typeset by Wessex Typesetters
(Division of The Eastern Press Ltd)
Frome, Somerset

Printed in Hong Kong

British Library Cataloguing in Publication Data
Bradby, David
Directors' theatre.—(Macmillan modern
dramatists).
1. Theatre. Directing
I. Title   II. Williams, David
792'.0233
ISBN 0–333–29424–5
ISBN 0–333–29425–3 Pbk

Contents

List of Plates

List of Plates

Editors' Preface

The *Macmillan Modern Dramatists* is an international series of introductions to major and significant nineteenth- and twentieth-century dramatists, movements and new forms of drama in Europe, Great Britain, America and new nations such as Nigeria and Trinidad. Besides new studies of great and influential dramatists of the past, the series includes volumes on contemporary authors, recent trends in the theatre and on many dramatists, such as writers of farce, who have created theatre 'classics' while being neglected by literary criticism. The volumes in the series devoted to individual dramatists include a biography, a survey of the plays, and detailed analysis of the most significant plays, along with discussion, where relevant, of the political, social, historical and theatrical context. The authors of the volumes, who are involved with theatre as playwrights, directors, actors, teachers and critics, are concerned with the plays as theatre and discuss such matters as performance, character interpretation and staging, along with themes and contexts.

BRUCE KING
ADELE KING

Acknowledgements

The help of the following has been invaluable in the course of our research and writing: Edward Braun, Howard Goorney, Oscar Lewenstein, Michel Bataillon, René Gaudy; Ludwik Flaszen, Ryszard Cieslak and Zygmunt Molik of the Polish Teatr Laboratorium; Richard Gough and the Cardiff Laboratory Theatre resource centre; Peter Brook, Nina Soufy, Bruce Myers and Yoshi Oida of the C.I.R.T., Paris; Georges Banu of the C.N.R.S., Paris; Michael Patterson, Ruth Walz and the Schaubühne, Berlin; Robert Wilson and the Byrd Hoffman Foundation, New York. Finally, our thanks to the two Rachels, to Anne Kilcoyne and to the people of Ortakent Köyü, S. Turkey.

Photos are reproduced courtesy of the following:

Roger Viollet – 1a–3
René Basset – 4a & b
Pierre Clavel – 5a & b
Bernand – 6

Acknowledgements

Michel Sarti – 7a & b
Polish Teatr Laboratorium – 14–16
Donald Cooper – 17–18
C.I.R.T. – 19a–21
Gilles Abegg – 22
Michel Dieuzaide – 23
Ruth Walz – 24–33
Byrd Hoffman Foundation – 34–40

The authors and publishers are grateful to the copyright holders listed above for permission to reproduce illustrations. Every effort has been made by the publishers to trace all copyright holders. In cases where they may have failed they will be pleased to make the necessary arrangements.

1
The Rise of the Director

The dominant creative force in today's theatre is the director. No longer just an organiser, the director is now considered an artist in his or her own right. Critics write of 'Brook's *Lear*', of 'Planchon's *Tartuffe*', ascribing to the director the role of author. It is a distinguishing feature of directors' theatre that here the director claims the authorial function even though he has not written the original play. Where he is working with a classic text, he will rearrange, cut and rewrite to fit his production concept. Many contemporary directors dispense with the writer completely: outstanding examples are the image-dramas of Tadeusz Kantor and of Robert Wilson, some of which contain almost no written text at all. Even in less extreme examples, such as the work of Roger Planchon and of Peter Stein, the director's contribution is the equivalent of that of an author, amounting to the development of a new stage idiom – he assumes the function of 'scenic writer'.

Despite assuming authorial function, the greatest directors are those who at the same time succeed in bringing out the talents of actors and playwrights. Several contemporary directors can claim to have achieved what Brecht did with the Berliner Ensemble: Joan Littlewood with Theatre Workshop, Ariane Mnouchkine with the Théâtre du Soleil and Peter Stein with the Schaubühne have all succeeded in forging companies whose name is as well-known as that of their director. Moreover, all these directors, besides devising their own productions, have been responsible for bringing the work of new playwrights to the stage. Others, such as Peter Brook and Jerzy Grotowski, have founded centres for research into the dynamics of the actor–audience relationship. Their work, like that of Robert Wilson, has led them to devise activities more often associated with psychotherapy than with theatre. They have become charismatic figures, saints for a secular age, valued for their insistence on pursuing their own vision despite the normal criteria of theatre practice.

The function designated by the word 'director' in today's theatre is not more than a century old. Between the end of the eighteenth and the end of the nineteenth century changes took place that transformed the established European theatre from a restricted medium catering for the needs of the court to a mass medium appealing to a variety of social groups. In the eighteenth century, despite the thriving popular entertainers who performed at fairs and similar occasions, the only established theatre companies were those working under the patronage of royalty. These companies enjoyed the privilege of a monopoly on spoken drama: not only was their income assured, but competition was banned. Such conditions generated a measure of shared agreement between actors and audiences concerning the function of theatre and the appropriate manner of staging plays. The modern director has opened up a space for himself by challenging these conventional assumptions and proposing new models of how and why theatre should operate within society.

The initiators of this development were the nineteenth-century actor–managers, who began to insist on careful rehearsal and a unified style for costumes and settings. Charles Kean's Shakespeare productions, for example, were much admired for their accuracy of historical and geographical detail. In the same period the theatre's commercial status was changing: as the old monopolies were dismantled it became possible for a new breed of theatre manager to make substantial sums of money from building and running theatres in Europe's bigger cities. As audiences increased in size and lost their former homogeneity, so the old consensus disappeared, to be replaced by an appetite for novelty. The most successful theatres were those whose managers were able to introduce spectacular innovations. Unable to deal with topics of political urgency, catering for audiences hungry for special effects (such as shipwrecks, erupting volcanoes and runaway trains), these managers gave more and more prominence to design. Opportunities for spectacle were assisted by the rapid development of stage technology, especially in the area of lighting. The old oil lamps were replaced in the 1820s by gas lighting and then, during the last two decades of the century, by electric lighting. As the stage technology grew more complex, so did the need for a stage manager (*régisseur* in French) to ensure that the various stage effects worked well together. By the end of the century it was common for one person, often the leading actor and manager of the company, to assume artistic responsibility for all aspects of a performance, and the word used to designate this function was 'producer' (French: *metteur en scène*), though Edward Gordon Craig called him the stage director and can thus be seen as the first person to use the word in its modern sense. By choosing it, he intended to emphasise the director's role as master of all the signifying practices peculiar to the stage – gesture and movement, sound, lighting, costume, design and speech. For the first part of the twentieth century, however, the term 'producer' was generally employed, to be replaced during the 1950s by the term 'director', perhaps influenced by film terminology.

By the end of the nineteenth century any social consensus as to the function of theatre had broken down, as had the monolithic structure of patronage that had formerly guaranteed a living wage for theatre workers. The first directors in the modern sense of the word, men such as Antoine and Stanislavski, were determined to find new ways of filling both these needs. They proposed to create a new consensus by issuing manifestoes and establishing subscription societies. In this way they hoped to gather a homogeneous audience, based not on class but on shared interest in art, and to share the burden of financial support among all their patrons. In the transition from the old to the new structures, the most influential figure was a man who combined elements of both the old-fashioned aristocratic patron and the new theatre director: Duke Georg II of Saxe-Meiningen, whose theatre company, founded in 1866, toured Europe between 1874 and 1890.

Duke Georg anticipated the development of theatre directing by seizing on the idea that all effects of the production should be subordinated to a single unifying artistic aim, with particular emphasis on the visual aspects of his productions. He made detailed sketches of how each scene of a play was to look, including the sets, the positions of the actors, the groupings of 'extras' and the movements they would need to make from one part of the stage to another. He was greatly helped when, in 1873, he appointed Ludwig Chronegk as his stage director and leader of rehearsals. Chronegk was a disciplinarian who insisted on punctuality at rehearsals and on the faultless learning of every move, even by non-speaking parts. Duke Georg's designs and Chronegk's rehearsal methods resulted in productions full of expressive details all harnessed to a single artistic vision. The crowd scenes in particular caught Antoine's attention when he saw the company on tour: he was impressed by the ability of even the 'extras' to project realistic characters without damaging the overall design of a scene.

Historical plays provided the Meininger with their greatest successes. For the production of *Julius Caesar*, 'not only the settings, based on the remains of the Roman forum, but statues, armour, weapons, drinking cups and the rest were all modelled faithfully on Roman originals'. Such keen interest in historical reconstruction was a mark of the age, though not totally original: English actors had attempted similar effects since John Philip Kemble in the late eighteenth century, and Duke Georg appears to have been influenced by Charles Kean's celebrated Shakespeare 'Revivals'.[1] Unlike Kemble or Kean, Duke Georg had the advantage of not being the star of his own productions, so he was able to retain an objective observer's eye and approached the task of historical reconstruction in a rigorously systematic fashion.

The new historical awareness of the nineteenth century certainly contributed to the emergence of the director, who was able to reinforce his claim to authority by developing the notion of the 'classic'. The modern director Roger Planchon has pointed out that in previous centuries it was assumed that to perform a play from the classical repertoire meant making a new adaptation: '*The Miser* only exists because Molière would not perform Plautus without rewriting him.' For Planchon, it was the idea of the classic that did most to bring the modern director into being:

> The emergence of the classic brings with it the birth of a dubious character. He presents himself as a museum curator; leaning on Molière and Shakespeare, he levers himself into a position where he is running the whole show. We may lament the fact, but the two things are linked: the birth of the classic gives power to the theatre director. In his hands the great theatres of the world become museums and justify their existence by producing *Oedipus*, *Hamlet*, or *The Miser*. A museum curator 'restores' works and puts them on show. And this is where the ambiguities begin. . . .[2]

There is some force in Planchon's argument that the modern director functions like a museum curator, an argument also advanced by Jonathan Miller: 'Why did the director emerge when he did? Why has his influence now become so strong? The obvious answer is that historical change has accelerated so much in the last fifty years that the differences between "now" and even a quite recent "then" are much more noticeable.'[3] The productions of the Meininger were a response to the birth of this enhanced historical awareness, as were the experiments of William Poel, who in 1894 set up an 'Elizabethan Stage Society' in England for the purpose of presenting Shakespeare's plays in uncut versions on a reconstructed Elizabethan stage. It soon became evident that such experiments, though producing fascinating results, could not succeed in their own terms, for the audience of the 1890s perceived Shakespeare differently from the Elizabethans, just as Shakespeare's picture of Julius Caesar's Rome was different from Duke Georg's. After a few decades, enthusiasm for historical reconstruction gave way to a realisation that each new period discovers new meanings in the works of the past and that historical reconstructions reveal more about the reconstructors than about the period they seek to revive. This is the source of the ambiguities mentioned by Planchon, for modern directors have frequently copied Duke Georg in claiming that their's is the most 'authentic' version ever staged of a given classic. In fact they are laying claims to a function more authorial than directorial, hence the debate about the legitimate extent of the director's power to adapt or 'restore' the classics.

For André Antoine, the most interesting aspect of Duke Georg's productions was their verisimilitude. Often described as the first modern director, Antoine also came to rely on productions of the classics in his later career, but when he set up his Théâtre Libre in 1887 he dedicated it to the performance of the new naturalist drama, seeking out and encouraging new playwrights. The theatre's name was intended to emphasise both its independence of spirit and its determination to offer an alternative to the superficialities of the commerical theatre available in Paris at that time. Antoine's innovations were often framed as rejections of the existing conventions and they bore on three fundamental aspects of a theatre's activity: its finances and audience relations; its style of design and production; its acting. Financially, the Théâtre Libre was set up as a subscription society. Because its performances were then 'private' it escaped censorship. Even more important was the financial independence this brought and the creation of a homogeneous audience. In production style, Antoine insisted on the detailed, realistic creation of setting and environment, 'for it is the environment that determines the movements of the characters, not the movements of the characters that determine the environment'. His ideal for interiors (not always put into practice) was to build the set first and to rehearse the play as if in a real room with four walls, 'without worrying about the fourth wall, which will later disappear so as to enable the audience to see what is going on'. He insisted that, instead of aiming chiefly to flatter and charm their audiences, his actors should devote all their powers to authentic character portrayal, introducing the notion, distinctly alien to French traditions, that acting was not only a matter of fine speaking: 'the best of our actors . . . know . . . that at certain moments of the action their hands, their back, their feet may all be more eloquent than a long speech'.[4]

Antoine's crusade against ham acting and cheap theatrical tricks would not have achieved such far-reaching results without the backing of Emile Zola. For some years Zola had been campaigning in favour of naturalism in the theatre, but the prevailing inauthenticity of acting and production styles made it hard to achieve the effect he desired, even with stage adaptations of his own novels. He condemned 'exaggerated gestures, movements made only for show, actors striking the stage with their heel' and many other tricks of the trade. He longed for a more truthful portrayal of character and dreamed of actors who would 'live the play rather than performing it'.[5] Antoine's aesthetic provided the necessary seriousness of approach and the willingness to confront contemporary social issues. Zola's active support became an important factor in the early success of the Théâtre Libre. In the previous decade he had published a torrent of articles in which he developed the idea that both literature and theatre had to adopt the experimental method of science if they were to recover their lost vocation as interpreters of contemporary society. He set out a programme for modern documentary writing in which the author would be no more than an intensely scrupulous observer of reality. This fitted well with Antoine's desire to establish the stage as a space of privileged authenticity, almost like a sociological laboratory. The illusion that theatre could operate according to strict scientific principles was short-lived, but the conception of the director as responsible for a laboratory of human relationships has become a key element in modern directors' theatre, finding its most complete expression in Grotowski's 'Laboratory Theatre'.

Konstantin Stanislavski was an admirer of both Antoine and the Meininger. When he and Nemirovich-Danchenko set up the Moscow Art Theatre in 1898, they aimed to create a consensus in their audience by insisting that 'the performance be treated as an artistic experience, not a social occasion – applause of entrances and exits to be discouraged';[6] indeed everything was to be subordinated to the aim of artistic unity in the productions. Particular attention was to be paid to the creation of Antoine's 'environment': they found it necessary to specify, against the current practice of day, that each production would have specially designed settings, properties and costumes. Stanislavski's use, or even abuse, of atmospheric detail in his productions is too famous to require comment: in his own lifetime Chekhov was already complaining of its excesses when applied to his own plays. The survival of Stanislavski's promptbooks makes it possible to study these productions in the finest detail, right down to the movements, gestures and expressions of individual performers.

The creation of a realistic environment in which to set the action was as much the work of Stanislavski's designer Simov as of Stanislavski himself. The aim of overall artistic unity dictates the closest possible collaboration between director and designer from the moment that work on a given production begins. This is a feature of much contemporary directors' theatre. Peter Brook, for example, has written that 'the earliest relationship is director/subject/designer. . . . The best designer evolves step by step with the director, going back, changing, scrapping as a conception of the whole gradually takes form.'[7] For all his meticulous control of every detail in his productions, however, Stanislavski ultimately concluded that the director's most important creative work was done with the actors. As an actor himself, struggling for a new quality of truth and authenticity in his art, Stanislavski was constantly preoccupied with the difference between the actor who relies on externals, 'going through the motions' of a part, and the one who manages to 'live' the part, to convince the audience that the emotions portrayed are not merely simulated, but real, thus provoking a similar emotional response in them.

By observing his own reflexes as an actor, he discovered that he was sometimes inspired to the point of feeling the appropriate emotions as if he were the character, whereas at other times he felt quite wooden. During the last thirty years or so of his life he devised a method for enabling the actor to train his emotional reflexes so as not to have to rely on haphazard inspiration. This method, which he called 'the System', has been Stanislavski's most enduring legacy to the art of directing. Within this method, the role of the director is as much that of a teacher as that of an artist. His role is to stimulate the emotional memories of his actors so that they can find, within their own past experience, feelings similar to those of the character they have to portray. He will devise situations, often by using improvisation, through which these memories may be stirred. Observing his actors, he becomes a sort of director

10

of conscience, firmly censuring those emotions or responses which are merely feigned, and helping the actor to build on moments of truthfulness. The aim is to create a framework of authentic moments, drawn from the actor's own inner life, which will then give life to his character. Through his writings and through his disciples in America, Stanislavski's influence has been enormous. There is hardly a director working in the theatre today who does not use relaxation or improvisation techniques with their origin in Stanislavski's System. The authority of many contemporary directors derives less from their artistic programme than from their force of personality and from their ability to establish a working relationship with their actors in which the actors believe that they can grow, emotionally and spiritually. Both Brook and Grotowski, among contemporary directors, exhibit this characteristic of the director as guru.

The influence of the naturalist stage directors Antoine and Stanislavski spread rapidly to other European countries, notably to Germany. In 1889 Otto Brahm set up his Freie Bühne in Berlin. Like Antoine, Brahm was dedicated to performing new plays, often picking those with a socialist slant and introducing new work by Hauptmann, Tolstoy, Strindberg and Zola. Antoine and Stanislavski's influence made itself felt more slowly in England, where J. T. Grein set up the Independent Theatre Society in 1891, modelling himself explicitly on Antoine but without enjoying the same success.

It was not, however, naturalism but the rival symbolist movement that gave rise to the first great theorist of directors' theatre: Edward Gordon Craig. In his writings on the art of the theatre, Craig formulated a prophetic vision of the director as the supreme theatre artist of the modern age, uniting all processes in a single creative enterprise:

> I am now going to tell you out of what material an artist of the theatre of the future will create his masterpieces. Out of ACTION, SCENE, and VOICE. Is it not very simple?
> And when I say *action*, I mean both gesture and dancing, the prose and poetry of action.
> When I say *scene*, I mean all which comes before the eye, such as the lighting, costume, as well as the scenery.
> When I say *voice*, I mean the spoken word or the word which is sung, in contradiction to the word which is read, for the word written to be spoken and the word written to be read are two entirely different things.[8]

This vision suggests a director bringing together and mastering all the different expressive idioms of the stage. In fact the practicalities of theatre work often defeated Craig; for his few successful productions he drew heavily on the pioneering work of the Swiss designer Adolphe Appia, who was the first to exploit the possibilities of electric lighting in the theatre. As the new electric systems and dimmer boards were installed during the last decades of the nineteenth century, Appia saw that the art of production could become not merely the art of establishing an appropriate environment, but the creation of a new spatial idiom, more like that of dance or music.

In responding so enthusiastically to the new possibilities opened up by Appia and others, yet achieving relatively little in practice, Craig demonstrated the fundamental paradox of directors' theatre. For the director must indeed be the orchestrator of all the expressive idioms of the stage, yet if he treats them exclusively as raw materials to be reshaped he misses the most important thing, which is that, however impressive his vision, it only comes to life through the creative work of the actors, designers and all others involved in the process.

This was something well understood by the Russian director Vsevolod Meyerhold. Meyerhold had been an actor with Stanislavski's company, so he understood the demands placed on a naturalistic actor. He believed that Stanislavski's method was mistaken, because, by putting so much emphasis on creating the illusion of reality, it was unable to exploit that most essentially theatrical quality: play. Meyerhold turned his attention to the traditional skills of the popular performer: clowning, acrobatics, juggling, mime. He also studied the *commedia dell'arte* and the conventions of oriental theatre. After the Russian Revolution he eagerly accepted the challenge to elaborate new forms of dramatic expression, developing a system of actor training known as 'biomechanics'. Reflecting both the eurhythmics of Emile Jaques-Dalcroze and the optimistic belief in scientific method, this was an attempt to develop the body's capacity for movement with machine-like precision. Where an actor was called upon to display emotion, he was to do so by selecting appropriate physical movements, not by miming an internal state, as in Stanislavski's theatre. In his approach to setting, Meyerhold discarded both realistic environments and symbolist evocations. With the help of constructivist designers, he employed sets that were entirely functional: the actor no longer played in front of or even within the set; he played *with* it. These sets were characteristically composed of frameworks with ramps, steps and platforms at different levels over which the actors ran, leapt or tumbled. In this way Meyerhold managed to integrate the elements of line, movement, colour, rhythm and space of which Craig had spoken.

Inevitably, since most playwrights had not written with Meyerhold's performance idiom in mind, he was obliged systematically to re-create the dramatic action in terms of forms, images, movements unsuspected by the author. Indeed, he was often accused of supplanting the author. He denied this charge but agreed that his work amounted to a redefinition of the director's function and this he expressed diagrammatically by saying that the director had traditionally seen himself as merely a privileged spectator arranging and perfecting the performance before it was shown to the public thus:[9]

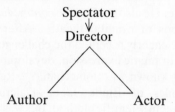

In his own work this relationship was no longer triangular but linear:

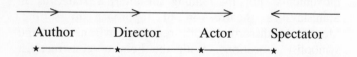

This conception of the director's role became one of the essential defining qualities of directors' theatre. All the directors considered in this book believe that the director must reformulate the author's work in terms of a fresh and living stage idiom, though not all would claim to place themselves so squarely between the actor and the author. Meyerhold's great contribution to directors' theatre was to insist that a unified artistic purpose was not enough; it was the director's responsibility to develop a style or idiom specific to the theatre within which every element became a significant bearer of meaning.

By the end of the first decade of this century the director's claim to artistic authority in the theatre was gradually becoming accepted. The man who did most to cement this authority was Jacques Copeau, who founded the Vieux-Colombier theatre in 1913, as an explicit attempt to renew the art of the French stage. He considered the Parisian theatre of the *belle époque* to be both corrupt and corrupting, offering its audiences nothing besides superficial bedroom farces or lavish spectacular shows whose only aim was sensational novelty. In their place he planned a theatre that was simple but inventive, one in which play and performance became an integrated whole. His repertoire was based on the classics, especially Molière and Shakespeare. He believed that, given faithful productions, inventive, sensitive acting and the minimum of special stage effects, these authors would reveal qualities of poetry and truth which contemporary theatre had lost sight of. He dreamed of developing a new performance vocabulary of modern types similar to the old masks of the *commedia dell'arte*, permitting actors to develop a supple, inventive commentary on contemporary life.

For a theatre that is now considered to have been so influential, the Vieux-Colombier had a remarkably short existence, playing for a total of only seven complete seasons between 1913 and 1924. Copeau's influence spread wide for two reasons. One was that two of these seasons were played in New York (1917–19), where the company was sent on a cultural mission. Its success was considerable and ensured rapid dissemination in the United States of Copeau's view of the role of the director. The second was that Copeau had also founded a theatre school alongside the theatre and he continued as its director after the closure of the theatre. The training given in this school began, like that of Meyerhold, by placing the emphasis almost solely on physical training and developing the expressive powers of the body. As the training progressed, other elements were introduced: study of art, philosophy and literature. The students were encouraged to cultivate the whole man, not just their performance technique, and to work for the group rather than as individuals. Almost all the leading directors in the French theatre of the next few decades were trained by Copeau or by former pupils of Copeau, and so, in the French-speaking world, his influence as a teacher equalled that of Stanislavski in Russia and America. Where Stanislavski stressed the director's work in helping the actor to free his inner resources, Copeau and his disciples emphasised the director's responsibility towards the European theatre tradition as a whole, giving renewed life to the plays of the classic repertoire and forming an ensemble of actors capable of group work and of generosity to one another. Copeau's charismatic influence was such that he imposed his vision of the director as a man embodying both artistic and moral authority on most of the succeeding generation of directors.

A less pedagogic view of the director's function, though an equally demanding one, was embodied by Copeau's contemporary Max Reinhardt. Reinhardt was an unashamed master of the spectacular production style, favouring enormous casts and productions in spaces not normally used for theatre performance. He is said to have preferred poor or incomplete plays, for these allowed him more scope to introduce effects of his own devising. Certainly one of his major successes was *The Miracle*, a wordless play by Karl Vollmöller. It was staged in London at the Olympia Hall with the audience seated facing one another as if in a great church, a central rostrum which could sink beneath the floor, and a hillside on rails. In a programme note for the play, Reinhardt defended the director's right to use whatever scenic means modern technology made available: 'Our standard must not be to act a play as it was acted in the days of its author. . . . How to make a play live in our time, that is decisive for us.'[10] With his love of the large-scale and the modern, it is not surprising that Reinhardt found a welcome in America, where he made a number of films. An interest in the application of technology to spectacle and a willingness to direct for both theatre and film have been a feature of many contemporary directors' work.

Reinhardt's work in Germany had not always been confined to grand spectacular productions. At his Kleines Theater from 1902 he produced intense small-scale dramas by such authors as Strindberg and Wedekind. As director of the Deutsches Theater in 1905, Reinhardt had opened a studio theatre next door as a second house, and there he directed a number of intimate productions significant in the flowering of the German Expressionist movement. Out of the Expressionist movement and its anguished protest against the mass slaughter of the First World War, there was to emerge a new concept of the director: as agitator for political change. The outstanding example is Erwin Piscator, who founded his Proletarian Theatre in 1920 with a manifesto which declared uncompromisingly that 'any artistic intention must be subordinated to the revolutionary purpose of the whole'. Piscator set out to create a political theatre which could speak directly to a working-class audience. He was constantly hampered in this aim by the fact that for most of his productions he had to rely on financial support from the very class whom he opposed: the

17

wealthy bourgeoisie. Nevertheless he succeeded in developing a new style of episodic presentation which borrowed from music-hall, political cabaret, film and documentary material of all kinds to create a composite picture not of a character or a story but of a political theme. In the mid 1920s he developed the use of multi-media presentation to give an account on stage of a whole historical period, for example the First World War in *The Good Soldier Schweik*, adapted from Hasek, or the first seven years of the Weimar Republic in *Hoppla, wir leben!* by Toller. The latter was performed on an enormous structure with many different playing areas, allowing for the presentation of a whole cross-section of society, often with different scenes taking place simultaneously, or a film projection juxtaposed with an acted scene.

Bertolt Brecht was able to learn from both Reinhardt and Piscator, since he was on the payroll of Reinhardt's Deutsches Theater as *Dramaturg* from 1924 to 1926 and also helped on several of Piscator's productions. He was clearly more impressed by Piscator, whose political aims he shared, and he later acknowledged the considerable debt he owed to him. But he nevertheless differed considerably from Piscator in his aims and methods. His main priority was to show individuals in a process of continual change: changed by their society and environment but also changing it in their turn. He felt that Piscator's emphasis on the mechanisation of the stage had led to the complex depiction of political circumstances appearing to crush the individuals caught up in them, and that he had paid too little attention to the actor. Brecht did not become the director of his own company until late in life, but his first work as a director was on Marlowe's *Edward II* in 1924 and his development as a director ran parallel to his writing, so that Brecht the director cannot be separated from Brecht the playwright. The first requirement of theatre for Brecht was that it should be *fun*. He claimed to have learnt most from the Munich dialect comedian Karl Valentin and admired his relation with his audience, based not on emotional identification but on amused detachment. He found the same detachment in a crowd at a sporting event and he wanted theatre audiences to be as alert to the finer points of the actor's craft as a sporting crowd is to the technique of a famous footballer. In pursuit of this vision of theatre, Brecht evolved his characteristic production style: the half curtain which did not attempt to hide all the preparations in progress behind it; the use of placards or screen projections to comment on the action; the non-naturalistic settings; the visible rows of stage lights. Props had to be as authentic as possible, but the imaginary 'fourth wall' and other tricks of illusionist theatre were sacrificed in the interests of clear demonstration.

Perhaps the most significant element of all in Brecht's peculiar production style was his refusal to resolve the contradictions of life on stage but to present them in all their stubborn reality. Rather than tell his audience *what* to think, he encouraged them (most of the time) simply *to think*. Hence the importance of what he termed the *Verfremdungseffekt* (alienation effect). This had a dual purpose: both to interrupt the flow of the story, emphasising its contradictory qualities, and to take the 'human social incidents to be portrayed and labelling them as something striking, something that calls for explanation, is not to be taken for granted, not just natural'.[11] When he became director of the Berliner Ensemble after the Second World War, he applied this method to his own plays, refusing to take anything for granted and quite willing to rewrite when necessary. In this company he tried to form a group whose leadership was collective, so as to ensure that

19

everybody's opinion was considered. This insistence on the need for democratic structures within the company itself has been a priority for many contemporary directors, especially Mnouchkine and Stein. Brecht's use of space and setting was particularly brilliant, involving eclectic borrowing from the work of almost all the directors so far mentioned. Carl Weber wrote that

> Brecht regarded design as of the highest importance, and had worked out his methods of handling it with his friend Caspar Neher. . . . He began with people, sketching the characters in relation to the given situation, and thus visualizing the blocking. When he and Brecht were satisfied with the sketches, they started to develop a set. For Brecht . . . the set was primarily a space where actors tell a certain story to the audience. The first step was to give the actor the space and architectural elements he needed; the next was to work out the set so it by itself would tell the audience enough about the play's story and contradictions, its period, social relations, and the like; the last step was to make it beautiful, light, 'elegant' as Brecht used to say.[12]

Brecht himself did not give much prominence to the director as such, seeing the two main tasks of theatre as that of the *Dramaturg*, whose responsibility was a clearly defined narrative, and the actors, whose responsibility was the characters. Nevertheless, his success in achieving a production style both delicate and complex is attested by the reactions of theatre people when the Berliner Ensemble was seen for the first time outside East Berlin in 1954. His influence was decisive for the development of Planchon, and it was an important element in the work of almost all the directors we shall be discussing. His work was

20

an inspiration to those directors, such as Mnouchkine and Stein, who helped to establish theatre collectives in the late 1960s, and in this case it was not simply his techniques that they learnt from, but his whole philosophy of theatre: what it was for and whom it was supposed to serve.

This was the major question raised by the other great prophet of the modern theatre, Antonin Artaud. Although he had little success in practical terms as a director, Artaud's collection of essays *The Theatre and its Double* (1938) has influenced the way directors are viewed, and view themselves, because of the all-embracing claims it makes for theatre, and for the director in particular. Artaud's favourite analogy for theatre was the plague. Like the plague, he wrote, theatre's effect should be that of a great collective nightmare, from which few would emerge unscathed but which would leave society somehow purged. Artaud's ideas, and the impact they have had, are indicative of a time of doubt, despair and the decline of religious belief. At such times people cast around for a priest-figure: someone who can speak with authority and immediacy, short-circuiting the elaborate codes of scientific or sociological discourse. Artaud claimed that the role of theatre, rightly understood, was to break through language and touch the well-springs of life. In this vision of theatre, the director becomes a sort of shaman, and it is not by chance that Peter Brook, searching for a definition of 'holy' theatre in his book *The Empty Space*, concludes with the evocation of a Haitian voodoo ceremony, in which invisible powers are made present in the persons of the participants.

In the last hundred years, then, the director has progressed from the role of simple stage manager to the position of central power in the theatre enterprise. His rise to power has been assisted by the complex set of historical–cultural factors to which we have alluded in the course of this introduction. As a result, directors have been in a position to do very much more than just direct plays and have assumed a variety of different functions: the prophet, teacher and founder of schools; the revolutionary agitator working for a change in the whole society; even the priest and organiser of sacred mysteries. In the process they have attracted strong criticism, especially when they have usurped the function of the playwright. The precise location of the dividing line between the creative responsibilities of the director and those of the writer is a problem that has preoccupied many of the directors studied in this book.

The most important change in theatre structures, contributing to the present power of the director, has been the change in patronage: most of today's major directors are funded by the state. Unlike the old aristocratic patrons, or even the subscription societies of the turn of the century, the modern capitalist state does not usually have clearly formulated artistic preferences. It may well have clear political imperatives, which a director ignores at his peril: Hitler's fascism forced both Brecht and Piscator into exile and Meyerhold died at the hands of the Stalinist state. Post-war capitalist states have mostly assumed a stance of tolerance. Although Littlewood was systematically starved of funds, directors such as Planchon, Brook, Stein and Mnouchkine have been able to insist on a degree of creative freedom while at the same time receiving large state subsidies. By and large the state has only been prepared to continue this funding for as long as a given director has enjoyed success at the box office.

Once he can persuade the state to fund him adequately, the modern director enjoys almost total control. The subsidy is often paid direct to him, so that his power over both actors and authors is as complete as that of nineteenth-century managers who hired or fired at whim. It was to this state of affairs that Ariane Mnouchkine referred when she said, 'remember that the director has already achieved the greatest degree of power he's ever had in history. And our aim is to move beyond that situation by creating a form of theatre where it will be possible for everyone to collaborate without there being directors, technicians and so on in the old sense.'[13] Paradoxically, it is those directors who have set out to diminish their own power in the company who have usually succeeded in creating the most exciting and also the most identifiable directors' theatre. It is the purpose of this book to investigate that process in seven particular cases, all representatives of a 'second generation', building on the achievements of the pioneers of the early twentieth century. The seven we have picked form a representative sample of post-war directors, each representing at least one aspect of the different directorial functions outlined in this introduction.

2
Joan Littlewood

Joan Littlewood's life as a director was marked by the determination to question all the established practices of the British theatre. Her great ambition was to make theatre once more a vital force in society in the same way as it had been for the Elizabethans: a focus both for popular fun and for political debate. Like Brecht, she was a charismatic personality nevertheless committed to collaborative working methods; like him, she developed a distinctive production style that grew organically from her political convictions; like him, her mature style was partly shaped by the agit-prop theatre of the 1930s. The significance of her work lies in her ability to form a company and through it to develop a theatre style that gave adequate and complex expression to those convictions formed in the left-wing struggles of the 1930s.

The story of Joan Littlewood's theatre begins in 1931 in Manchester, three years before she herself arrived there. This was the year when a group called the Red Megaphones was set up by a sixteen-year-old working class boy called

24

Jimmy Miller (who later changed his name to Ewan MacColl). Miller had grown up in a background of trades union militancy, joining the Young Communist League, writing articles, songs and lampoons for factory newspapers. In 1931 there were strikes in the Lancashire cotton industry directed against the proposed introduction of the eight-loom system. Miller wrote some short sketches which the Red Megaphones performed at strike centres, adapting the German form of short spoken chorus. These were partly improvised, changing to suit the precise political circumstances of the day. 'The job was to get people to do it smartly, to be able to move into position, to perform it and be away before the cops got onto you.'[1]

Soon the group became more ambitious. They were convinced that to offer a real alternative to the middle-class theatre of the day they had to develop a new style of acting and production: a theatre of mixed means, in which the actors would be able to sing, dance and act with equal facility. Drawing on the resources of the Manchester reference library, teaching themselves the rudiments of French and German, they studied the work of Appia and Craig, the German Expressionists and the great Russian directors: Stanislavski, Meyerhold, Vakhtangov. Particularly important was the enthusiam of Alf Armitt, their lighting specialist, who put his researches to good use by constructing a small transportable lighting rig which could be plugged in anywhere (even, on one occasion, hitched up to a trolley-bus cable).

In 1934 they decided to perform indoors, changed their name to Theatre of Action and issued a manifesto which announced that they would perform only plays expressing the lives and struggles of the workers. It was at this point that Joan Littlewood joined the group. Born and brought up in Stockwell, London, Littlewood also came from a poor background with militant trades union connections, but her education had been more privileged than Miller's since she had attended a South London convent school and the Royal Academy of Dramatic Art, where she was financed by a London County Council scholarship. She had reacted strongly against the cosy middle-class world of the English stage between the wars and had travelled to Paris to discover more about continental theatre. On her return she took a job at Rusholme Repertory Theatre in Manchester, where she was also able to work on a BBC radio documentary about the building of the Mersey Tunnel. It was through this that she met Jimmy Miller (Ewan MacColl) and joined Theatre of Action.

Her first activity with Theatre of Action was to start movement classes. She and MacColl decided to make an adaptation of a naturalistic anti-war play called *Hammer*, turning it into a stylised production with a new title: *John Bullion – A Ballet with Words*. This production, with its close integration of speech, movement and lighting, bore the stamp of Meyerhold's influence. Like the Russian director, Littlewood wanted her actors to be as supple as acrobats so that a specifically theatrical form of physical expression could be developed – one that was based not on close imitation of everyday life but on traditional forms of popular expression: the clown show, the circus, the carnival.

The Theatre of Action's programme led to disputes with the local Communist Party and the disintegration of the group. Littlewood and MacColl left Manchester for London, hoping to take up invitations to study theatre in Moscow, but their visas failed to come through, so, in 1936, they returned to Manchester and formed Theatre Union, which also issued a manifesto. While again stressing that theatre must join in the battles being fought between oppressor and oppressed, this made larger claims, placing its work in the tradition of the Ancient Greek, Elizabethan and Spanish theatres as well as those of Molière and Schiller. The repertoire was more ambitious, too, including Hans Schlumberg's *Miracle at Verdun* (a favourite of left-wing theatres in France at that time), Lope da Vega's *The Sheepwell* and Piscator's adaptation of *Schweik*, for which they used back-projection.

Participation in Theatre Union involved a whole programme of education. Though more militant, it resembled Copeau's ideal: not merely a training in movement and voice, but also an education in political thought, dramatic literature, theatre design and technology. All of these found expression in *Last Edition* (1940), a 'living newspaper' based on the researches of all members of the company, who then worked together on methods of theatrical expression. The thrust of the production was to express, by illustration from recent events, the view that war was a disaster for the working class, who were called upon to sacrifice themselves by the very people who exploited them in peace time. It was performed on a stage running round three sides of the audience and used a wide variety of performance styles. In order to avoid the censorship laws then in operation, *Last Edition* was played in 'club' performances, but this did not prevent Littlewood and MacColl being taken to court and bound over for two years, with a surety of £20 each.

The war caused the group to disperse, but a small nucleus continued the educational work that had been such an important part of Theatre Union's activities. Littlewood continued to work for BBC radio during the war, and thus maintained her contacts with people in Manchester, particularly with Gerry Raffles, whom she had met in 1940 and who was to be her companion until his death in 1975.

As soon as demobilisation began, Littlewood was writing to former Theatre Union members urging them to reunite, and in spring 1945 a nucleus met together to plan a new theatre for the post-war years. Thirty-six years later, Howard Goorney, who was one of that nucleus, published a fine account of Theatre Workshop's history, together with comments by a large number of company members.[2] His compilation has provided the documentation for this assessment of Littlewood as a director.

Although Littlewood was always the main source of energy behind the group, Theatre Workshop was not set up as her company but as a workers' co-operative in which all drew the same salary and all had an equal voice in decision-making. Later Littlewood was to declare 'I do not believe in the supremacy of the director, designer, actor or even of the writer. It is through collaboration that this knockabout art of theatre survives and kicks.'[3] This principle of collaboration was at the very heart of her project as a theatre director. It was a novel one, in contrast both with the habits of the English stage and with the practice of the continental directors whom she followed, but it is a principle shared by every one of the post-war directors studied in this book.

Theatre Workshop's first production was *Johnny Noble*, written by Ewan MacColl and described as a 'ballad opera' with traditional tunes. It made inventive use of light and sound, as well as stylised, semi-dance movement to tell the story of a young merchant seaman living through the events of the past dozen years. The opening sequence demonstrates clearly the self-consciously theatrical nature of the company's work:

IST NARRATOR (*singing*). Here is a stage.

Joan Littlewood

2ND NARRATOR (*speaking*). A platform twenty-five feet
by fifteen feet.

1ST NARRATOR (*singing*). A microcosm of the world.

2ND NARRATOR (*speaking*). Here the sun is an amber
flood and the moon a thousand-watt spot.

1ST NARRATOR (*singing*). Here shall be space
Here we shall act time.

2ND NARRATOR (*speaking*). From nothing everything will
come.

1ST NARRATOR (*singing*). On this dead stage we'll make
Society appear.[4]

As this extract shows, the company established from the
outset a very particular relationship with its audience. It
was very much the same as that demanded by Brecht: not
the dull, emotionless style that passes for 'Brechtian', but
something vital, if contradictory. The opening clearly aims
to distance its audience while at the same time inviting it to
appreciate the theatrical skill about to be displayed, rather
as a sporting crowd might appreciate athletic technique.
But, in what follows, the audience, instead of being kept at
a distance, is immediately drawn imaginatively into the
world of Johnny Noble, and the performance frequently
established moments of lyrical or emotional intensity,
though these would, in turn, be interrupted by a reminder
of harsh realities. In short, the play lived up to the aims
stated in Theatre Workshop's manifesto:

> The great theatres of all times have been popular
> theatres which reflected the dreams and struggles of the
> people. The theatre of Aeschylus and Sophocles, of
> Shakespeare and Ben Jonson, of the Commedia
> dell'Arte and Molière derived their inspiration, their
> language, their art from the people.

29

We want a theatre with a living language, a theatre which is not afraid of the sound of its own voice and which will comment as fearlessly on Society as did Ben Jonson and Aristophanes.

Theatre Workshop is an organisation of artists, technicians and actors who are experimenting in stage-craft. Its purpose is to create a flexible theatre-art, as swift moving and plastic as the cinema, by applying these recent technical advances in light and sound, and introducing music and the 'dance theatre' style of production.[5]

The first paragraph may be accused of being tendentious, but the second and third paragraphs provide a remarkably clear definition of Littlewood's aims as a director, aims which she was largely to achieve in the two decades following the war.

Johnny Noble, in a double bill with *The Flying Doctor*, adapted from Molière, was taken on tour round schools and community halls in the North West. For Littlewood there were only fruitful contradictions to be found in the pairing of a Molière farce and a piece of modern social comment. This was equally evident from the company's next two shows, Lorca's poetic farce *The Love of Don Perlimplin for Belisa in his Garden* and Ewan MacColl's *Uranium 235*, a play about atomic energy from the point of view both of scientific discovery and of social morality.

In 1946 Theatre Workshop moved its permanent base to Ormesby Hall, outside Middlesbrough, where they lived a communal life of training and rehearsing which again recalls, in some respects, the retreat of Copeau's group to Burgundy in the twenties. The difference was that Theatre Workshop's period at the Hall was only a brief interlude between hectic tours, and the atmosphere there was constantly enlived by an inventive sense of fun. The company was joined by Jean Newlove, who had trained and worked with Rudolf Laban and who was able to teach Laban movement systematically. Movement and relaxation exercises became a regular feature of the company's life, with the result that acting-parts of all kinds were approached primarily through an analysis of body movement. Weekend schools were offered, with workshops run by Littlewood, MacColl and Newlove.

But a company of this kind could not remain for long in a country mansion. In 1948 it returned to Manchester, though it continued its policy of touring until 1953, when it settled at Stratford in East London. The company that had come together after the war remained largely unchanged during the first post-war decade and many of its members have since expressed the conviction that this was the greatest learning experience of their lives. The work was genuinely experimental: each new production was an opportunity to try out new combinations of text, sound, light, movement. There was less emphasis on the study of earlier directors and more on the development of skills within the company, and this was to lead to the emergence of an identifiable Theatre Workshop idiom. It was through discoveries made by actors, director, designer, all working together, that the performance would gradually take shape. Howard Goorney recalls, 'words were rarely the starting point, even when rehearsing a classic; and in the case of a new play, the script was a long way from being finalised. The approach would usually be through the movement of the characters, exploring their relationships and the atmosphere of the play, moving only gradually towards the dialogue.'[6] Movement and improvisation were the key to Littlewood's working method from the beginning. As her confidence developed, she was to become more, not less, insistent on their value.

The type of staging was adjusted to suit each play. For *The Flying Doctor* a round platform, 12 feet in diameter was used, supporting a wall, a door and a window; it was revolved by two actors in full view of the audience. This use of a revolve was perhaps a device borrowed from Piscator; it was one to which Littlewood was to return in her 1954 production of *Schweik*. The value of a revolve used in this way is that it allows for the use of three-dimensional working elements such as doors and windows, while stressing the artificial, theatrical context of the whole performance. The alternative, a box set, apart from being less easy to transport, places more constraints both on the actors' use of space and on the imaginative appeal to the audience. John Bury was developing a flexible use of lighting to go with the openness of the staging. Different levels were frequently employed, with ramps or steps to connect them, and productions such as *Richard II* or *Arden of Faversham* (both 1954) reproduced the upper and lower levels of the Elizabethan stage.

This flexible use of space was reinforced by imaginative use of movement. David Scase, who performed in *Johnny Noble*, recalled Littlewood's direction of a scene on a boat:

I was sitting on the deck and another man was standing. I was taking the pitch and toss of the boat, the forward and aft movement, whereas the man who was standing was taking the roll of the boat, starboard to port. So in fact, we were side by side, moving in slightly different directions. On the side of the stage, to emphasise that, she had the green and port light going up and down with the ship moving at sea. This was all there was on stage, two actors, two lights and the sound of the engine going

1a.

1b. *The Good Soldier Schweik* (1954): A small revolving stage used in conjunction with fixed scenery

'debum . . . debum . . . debum . . .' People have told me they were literally feeling seasick at the end of the scene. Now this was genius.[7]

Perhaps the most daring stroke of all during this period was the Atomic Ballet in *Uranium 253*, a demonstration, by means of mime, movement and dance, of how splitting the atom releases energy. The text of this piece has recently been published along with others from the same period.[8]

The acting styles employed were as flexible as those developed for design and movement, relying particularly on the study of popular farce going back to the *commedia dell'arte*. The choice of a Molière farce gave opportunities for such work, especially as the play was adapted using additional material by the seventeenth-century *commedia* actor Domenico Biancoletti. Although the actors never played in masks, they were encouraged to aim for the same style of acting as that employed by the masked actor who, deprived of visual subtleties, has to make every gesture speak volumes. Like Meyerhold, Littlewood believed that the actions developed by people at work possessed their own qualities of economy and poetry, which could be very expressive on the stage. She included such actions wherever possible, as in the sequence of hauling in the nets in *Johnny Noble*. But as with Meyerhold this belief carried over into the portrayal of more private, individual feelings on stage. She would always encourage actors to find a movement which *conveyed* the emotion rather than a state which *imitated* it. It was perhaps for this reason that, like Brecht, she was fond of casting against type. For Littlewood, an actor who looked exactly right for the part would need to work less hard and therefore produce a less interesting performance than an actor who did not fit one's image of the character. The acting style fostered by

Littlewood could thus be described as broad and highly gestural, full of energy and movement. It could be summed up in the one word people used most frequently in descriptions or reviews: 'vital'.

After seven and a half years touring, living only on box-office receipts, always in debt, there came a point when something had to change. The decision was taken to give up touring and to take up permanent residence in a theatre, but it would nevertheless be a theatre in a working-class district: the Theatre Royal at Stratford East. This decision led to the first big split in the company. Ewan MacColl felt that Stratford East was too near the centre of London and that Theatre Workshop would not be strong enough to fight against the gravitational pull of the West End. In a way, he was to be proved right. The move had been encouraged by Gerry Raffles, who could see that, in order to develop as a director, Littlewood had to have her own theatre. Having a fixed home did not at first alter Theatre Workshop's status as a co-operative in which decisions were taken collectively and all drew the same salary. Peggy Soundy, who formed the Theatre Royal Supporters' Club, recalled the emphasis on collective work, remarkably similar to that of Ariane Mnouchkine's Théâtre du Soleil twenty years later: 'Joan was obsessed with everyone being completely versatile. If you wanted to act, write, direct or whatever, first of all you had to paint and decorate and use a vacuum cleaner.'[9]

The process of learning and experimentation continued as the company had to broaden its repertoire. It performed its first plays by Shaw, O'Casey and Chekhov and also began to perform Shakespeare and Jonson regularly. 1954 saw the first performances for over 300 years of the anonymous Elizabethan domestic tragedy *Arden of Faversham*. In her versions of the Elizabethan dramatists,

Littlewood's fundamental approach was the same as in her production of modern works. She defended a modern-dress *Macbeth* in 1957 by saying, 'If Shakespeare has any significance today, a production of his work must not be regarded as a historical reconstruction but as an instrument still sharp enough to provoke thought, to extend man's awareness of his problems, and to strengthen his belief in his kind.'[10]

Littlewood's emphasis in her productions of the classics was always on discovering the popular voice she believed to have been the essential ingredient in the greatness of playwrights such as Shakespeare and Jonson. In her view this meant rediscovering the urgency of their plays and making them sharply relevant to today. Her methods in pursuit of this aim did not generally involve ruthless updating but were more complex: detailed study of the period and historically authentic costume for *Richard II* and *Arden of Faversham*, for example. Like Brecht, she insisted that the actors must have a profound historical understanding if they were to make a play set in the past truly relevant to today. For *Richard II*, as Howard Goorney recalls, Littlewood worked through a process of exercises aimed at developing the enmity between the characters, the sudden outbreaks of violence, the suspicions, the ever-present fear of the knife in the back. This last image became a visual key to the production as Littlewood encouraged her actors to imagine what it was like to be an English nobleman at Richard's court: 'Pretend that stretching out before you is your future, your sons and their sons in a great long line. Behind you is a man with a dagger, about to plunge it into your back.' For the more cartoon-like characters of *Volpone*, a different style of playing was appropriate, more in the tradition of the *commedia*. Littlewood chose contemporary Italy as a setting for this production, embracing every available stereotype, creating a satire of post-war society at once hilarious and corrosive.

Looking back at the comments by contemporary critics, it is clear that the preconceptions of the period about performing Shakespearian theatre prevented them from seeing the particular skills of Littlewood's direction. Shakespeare for them meant fine poetry finely spoken. If there was some added pageantry in the production, so much the better, but it had to be seen as strictly secondary to the text. From this perspective it was impossible to appreciate the revolutionary (in every sense) qualities of Littlewood's methods. For the same reasons, it is possible to understand the rapturous reception given to *Arden of Faversham* and *Volpone* at the Paris International Festival in May 1955. The previous year, at the first Paris Festival, critics and theatre professionals alike had been overwhelmed by the visit of the Berliner Ensemble. Here they had discovered a company with a high level of ensemble acting and a performance style proceeding from Brecht's Marxist analysis of social relations. It combined great attention to concrete detail with inventive use of gesture and group movement. The experience was to influence styles of acting and production in France for the next fifteen years. A year later the same critics were delighted by Theatre Workshop because they found in its performances the same qualities of inventiveness, vitality and gestural clarity. No doubt their appreciation of these productions was positively aided by the fact that they were given in a foreign language. The result of this was that the gestural qualities emerged all the more clearly, and the worry of English critics about the speaking of the verse was not so important a factor. The same considerations explain why, the following year, Ewan MacColl's *Good Soldier*

Schweik, which had been dismissed by some London critics as vulgar, was again highly praised in Paris. The self-consciously theatrical style of production was appreciated for its coherence and inventiveness, not dismissed merely because it broke the rules of naturalistic decorum.

Littlewood's work presented distinct similarities with that of the most vigorous young French director of the period: Roger Planchon. Planchon's *Henry IV* (1957) was performed in a style very similar to that evolved by Littlewood for *Arden of Faversham* or *Richard II*. They shared a particular combination of violence and slapstick, which seemed shockingly new to many critics. The two directors had arrived at this style through a determination both to reflect the concrete realities of class conflict and to develop a new means of expression derived from popular traditions. In 1954 Planchon had produced Marlowe's *Edward II*, which Theatre Workshop was to perform in 1956. There were even similarities in design and use of space. For *Edward II*, John Bury designed a map of England which covered the whole stage floor, set on a ramp. At the end of the play Edward died sprawled across this symbolic and yet very concrete representation of his lost land. For Planchon's *Henry IV*, the set design also consisted of vast maps of England, though they were hung rather than spread on the stage, and the production also emphasised the basis of the struggle for power in territorial ownership.

It is not surprising that there should be similarities between the work of these directors. Both were motivated by the same desire to develop a new production style, both flexible and exciting, that would make the theatre accessible as well as meaningful to working-class audiences. Both were attempting to perform new dramatists as well as the classics. Both approached the problems of stage direction from a Marxist perspective and both were pioneers in introducing Brecht's work to the West European theatre. It was in 1955 that Littlewood put on the English première of *Mother Courage*, at the Barnstaple Festival. She had received permission to perform the play through the intervention of Oscar Lewenstein, who had convinced Brecht that Littlewood had all the qualities of an English Helene Weigel and could be depended on to avoid sentimentalising the character. Carl Weber came over from the Berliner Ensemble to make suggestions and to supervise the progress of rehearsals. In the meantime, Littlewood had cast another actress in the role of Mother Courage, so as to have more freedom to direct. Weber reported this back and Brecht threatened to withdraw the permission, so she took on the role again. Weber had brought with him Brecht's model book and photographs of his Berliner Ensemble production but Littlewood was incapable of working to a pre-established model: it undermined the very foundation of her working method. Inevitably there were arguments between her and Weber and in the end Raffles had to bar Weber from attending rehearsals. The production bore the marks of this unsettled preparation process. Although there was a good sturdy cart and the realities of poverty and war were presented with clarity, there was none of the lightness and humour recommended by Brecht. The performances were not well received, the production did not transfer to Stratford East, and it was the last time the English director who in so many ways resembled Brecht was to produce one of his plays.

In the opinion of many who worked with Joan Littlewood, 1955 marked the high point in her career. After ten years of shared experience her company had reached high standards of ensemble playing and spontaneity. One of Littlewood's most characteristic (and most feared) qualities as a director was her ability to push people up to and beyond their limits, refusing to let them get away with second best. Working with this kind of a director can be exhilarating but also exhausting. After the 1955 visits to Paris and Barnstaple a number of the founder members of Theatre Workshop left the company; from this time on Littlewood was never able to work again for a long period with a stable team. She found this depressing, and appears to have been less demanding of her actors in the late 1950s and 1960s.

Back at Stratford East she continued to promote her idea of theatre as a community service. She echoed Vilar's statement that theatre was as important to society as the other public services, such as health and education. Vilar paid the company a visit in 1956 and had high praise for its *Edward II*. The major difference between the two remained that Littlewood still had no significant subsidy, while her French counterpart was handsomely supported. The failure of the post-war Labour government to develop a policy for the arts that would have encouraged Theatre Workshop and groups like it had serious consequences for theatre in Britain. Even more serious was the failure of the trades union movement to support Littlewood's work in the 1950s. Naturally, she had expected opposition from those in entrenched positions. She might also have expected some support from others by way of compensation. But the support was sporadic and the opposition was particularly frank. It came from two main quarters: the Arts Council and the Lord Chamberlain. The Arts Council, despite its supposed political neutrality, consistently failed to subsidise Littlewood at the level she deserved. This is not simply a judgement made with the benefit of hindsight; it was quite clear to objective observers at the time, such as Graham Greene, who in 1958 offered to contribute £100 if nine others would follow his lead, to replace the £1000 that had just been withdrawn by the Arts Council. The Lord Chamberlain was the bane of all live theatre until 1968, when his duties as censor were abolished. Until that date every play had to be passed by him before it could be licensed for public performance. This posed particular difficulties for a director, such as Littlewood, who worked through improvisation and believed in making changes during the run of a show so as to keep it alive for the actors, since any change made to the text that had been seen by the Lord Chamberlain rendered her liable to prosecution.

Joan Littlewood's work as a director always depended on the belief that theatre can only function properly as a collaborative creation. This belief was expressed with great clarity in an open letter to the theatre journal *Encore* in 1961:

> No one in mind or imagination can foresee what a play will become until all the physical and intellectual stimuli, which are crystallised in the poetry of the author, have been understood by a company, and then tried out in terms of mime, discussion and the precise music of grammar; words and movement allied and integrated. The smallest contact between characters in a remote corner of the stage must become objectively true and relevant. . . . Only a company of artists can do this.[11]

After the departures in 1955, she therefore set about rebuilding her company of artists. With Ewan MacColl no longer part of the team, Littlewood was on the look-out for a new writer with whom to collaborate. Her policy of always reading manuscripts submitted to the theatre enabled her to spot the potential contained in a script by Brendan Behan, writer and convict, which drew on his experiences of prison life to construct a funny but emotionally hard-hitting plea against the death penalty: it portrayed life and conditions in a prison during the twenty-four hours leading up to an execution. For this play, *The Quare Fellow*, Littlewood had to employ a more naturalistic style than usual, but her working method followed the same pattern: the actors began by exploring, through improvisation and any other means available, the realities of prison life. Only after this introductory work was the script introduced, together with its author, who cut or rewrote according to suggestions made in rehearsals. He summed up his delight at these methods in a curtain speech on the first night, when he announced that the company had performed a better play than he had written.

This production was Littlewood's first unqualified success with the London critics. Bernard Levin described it as 'a marvellous combination of passion and humour which dwarfs anything else to be seen at present in London, West or East'; for Kenneth Tynan it was 'a model of restraint, integrity and disciplined naturalism'. As well as showing how Littlewood could recognise and nurture a new play-writing talent, it also demonstrated that her working method was sufficiently flexible and controlled to develop the style appropriate for the play. Behan's second play, *The Hostage*, written in even closer collaboration with the company, resulted in a show more typical of its ebullience, with songs and dances as well as plenty of political comment. If Howard Goorney's account is to be believed, it started with Behan regaling the cast for hours with anecdotes and songs. After this they would improvise, develop situations and characters. Finally Behan would be cajoled or bludgeoned into sitting down and writing dialogue, which would again be subject to changes. The play opened in 1958 and was an even greater success with the critics. It was invited to the Paris Festival in April 1959 and then transferred to Wyndham's Theatre, where it ran for more than a year. The profits returned to the Theatre Royal helped to supplement the meagre Arts Council grant of £1000 that the company was now receiving, but this meant that the cast was not available for work at Stratford East (Littlewood had insisted on the original cast being used). She therefore had, once again, to recruit and train a whole new company for her next show. This was a process that was to repeat itself five times over the course of the next three years. Financially, she could not afford to turn down the offer of a West End transfer, yet on each occasion she had to see the disappearance of the company that was the very cornerstone of her art. Raffles summed up the whole frustrating situation with brilliant brevity: 'We kept making drives towards the trade unionists and ending up among the aristocrats.'[12] Other plays to transfer during this period were Shelagh Delaney's *A Taste of Honey*, Frank Norman's *Fings Ain't Wot they Used t'be*, Wolf Mankowitz's *Make me an Offer* and Stephen Lewis's *Sparrers Can't Sing*. All of these were extensively cut and rewritten in the course of rehearsals, to the fury of some authors and to the delight of others.

All the important aspects of Littlewood's directorial style came together in her last major production for Theatre Workshop: *Oh What a Lovely War!* (1963). Since this production has proved to have a vigorous after-life, it provides a convenient opportunity for a summing-up. The starting point for the show was a radio feature by Charles Chilton on the songs that had been popular during the 1914–18 war. Raffles had the idea of building a performance around the songs, and Littlewood's aim was to trace the social and political background of the war. This was achieved by dividing up the task of research among members of the company, who would then meet up again regularly to pool their findings. The material drawn on included factual data from official records (much of it then only recently available, because of the fifty-year rule on official secrets), eye-witness accounts, and the work of historians such as A. J. P. Taylor, who dedicated his history of the war (1963) to Joan Littlewood. This method of creating a play has since become widespread and there are many examples to show how difficult it is to ensure the emergence of a good finished product. The clarity and brilliance of *Oh What a Lovely War!* must certainly be attributed in large part to Joan Littlewood and to her mastery of method and materials.

The play achieved its effects entirely by means of ironic contrast and counterpoint. Suspicious as ever of first-degree naturalism, Littlewood used the device of a pierrot troupe, the Merry Roosters, to present the play. The Merry Roosters were a real company, whose shows holidaymakers of the 1914–18 period had been able to see; the songs in the play were the popular songs of the day which doubtless they would have sung. With its roots in both clowning and popular ballad traditions, the format of the pierrot show provided Littlewood with a chance to exploit her feel for popular forms of entertainment. All the soldiers in the play wore some element of the pierrot costume, whether they were portraying senior officers at a ball or men dying in the trenches. The sharp discrepancy between this frivolous costume and the deadly realities evoked in the play was the first and most obvious of the structural contrasts. The second lay in the setting, which consisted of large screens for projections, leaving the stage almost entirely bare. Onto these screens were thrown

2a. *Oh What a Lovely War* (1963): Bayonet drill
sequence in Act I

images, contemporary photographs of First World War
soldiers, which both anchored the play in the reality of the
Flanders mud and contrasted with the Merry Roosters on
stage. In addition, a light-screen of the type used to flash up
news bulletins was placed high up running across the width
of the stage. In a few crucial scenes this screen carried the
terrifying facts of individual battles, e.g. 'NOVEMBER . . .
SOMME BATTLE ENDS . . . TOTAL LOSS 1,332,000 MEN . . . GAIN
NIL'.

Littlewood's genius for the use of movement also

2b.   *Oh What a Lovely War*: Ball sequence in Act II

contributed much to the show. Here again there was a sharp contrast between the Edwardian dance routines of pierrots and the aggressive movements required of soldiers. The two things were brought together with horrifying effect in a scene, played like an Irish jig, in which an Irish regiment was seen attacking so effectively and gaining so much ground that it came under artillery fire from its own side. Certain scenes were used to build up an intensely realistic image of life in the trenches, while others aimed to distance the audience by various alienating devices. One of the most successful was the scene of the church parade, in which, to the tune of 'What a friend we have in Jesus', the men sing about what they would do 'When this lousy war is over'. The songs of the period, such as 'We don't want to lose you, but we think you ought to go' were also used ironically to counterpoint the real horror of the trenches and to comment on the utter superficiality of those responsible for the war effort at home.

The sharpest contrast of all, and the one most responsible for hostile comment, was that between officers and men. The men were portrayed as lambs driven to the slaughter (literally in one scene), unable to control their destiny and yet facing up to intolerable hardships in a spirit of courage, humour and comradeship. Prominence was given to a scene portraying the fraternisation of British and German troops in no man's land on Christmas Eve 1915 in order to demonstrate (as had *Last Edition* in 1940) the international solidarity of the working class. This was a powerful scene, showing the beginning of friendship between British and Germans being rapidly squashed by shells being fired onto them in no man's land: those who had remained behind the lines had a vested interest in the continuation of the war. The officers and war profiteers were portrayed in complete contrast to the men. They were hypocritical, self-centred and interested only in what they could make out of the war. The researches conducted by the company into the period had left them in no doubt that the First World War was essentially a trade war, a struggle for access to markets, and the scenes showing civilians and members of the officer class attempted to put across this interpretation. Those who accused the show of being simplistic missed the point. Its primary aim was not to explain the causes of the war but to reveal the enormity of what had happened. In this it was entirely successful and audiences left the Theatre Royal in a state of shock.

Because of its reliance on sentimental songs of the period, the play has one danger: if the production is not sharp enough to throw up the various contrasts on which it depends, it may at times be swamped by the sentimental nostalgia of the songs. Littlewood was extremely alive to this danger, as Murray Melvin recalled: 'The whole point was to make war ugly. If a scene came over as being too attractive Joan would make us start again. "No", she'd shout, "you'll have them joining up."'[13] Yet for the transfer to the West End the thrust of the play was already blunted by a reprise of jolly songs at the end of the show, and, by the time it had been turned into a wide-screen film (directed by Richard Attenborough), sentiment had almost entirely taken over from protest. There was no trace of ugliness left and even the striking last shot, as the camera pulled back to reveal a whole hillside covered with graves, was beautiful.

For a variety of reasons, *Oh What a Lovely War!* was Littlewood's last completely successful production, although she mounted an impressive *Henry IV* at the Edinburgh Festival in 1964, with the two parts condensed into one evening and played in a mixture of styles and costumes. The critics did not like it, complaining, perhaps

3. *Oh What a Lovely War*: The pierrots perform a
    sugary song: 'Row, row, row'

rightly, that the company was not clear enough about what
it was trying to do. After this, she busied herself with
projects to try to fight off 'redevelopment' of Stratford East
and preserve the community life around the Theatre
Royal: a children's playground and a 'Fun Palace',
conceived as a sort of adventure playground for all ages.
When Raffles died in 1975 she went to live in France and
ceased theatre work altogether.

Littlewood's influence on the British stage has been

incalculable. Actors who worked with her invariably say that they never learned so much nor felt so alive. Directors and designers, from Peter Hall and John Bury at the National Theatre downwards, all acknowledge their debt to her. For Stanley Reynolds, writing in *The Guardian* (25 June 1984), 'the theatre you see today is the theatre that Joan Littlewood created'. Harold Hobson agreed with this assessment, explaining,

> Joan broke up the fabric of the British theatre. She, to a certain extent, disorganised it out of its old forms and began an internal revolution in the theatre in the way that plays were produced and the sort of plays that were produced. Also in the way they were written and in the way directors and players co-operated with the author. I doubt if there would have been any fringe without Joan.[14]

This well expresses Littlewood's achievement, since it states her concerted influence over every aspect of the theatre process. Her greatness lay in her total vision of what theatre could and should be. Her refusal to follow the established paths and conventional wisdoms produced failures as well as successes: had she been less stubborn, she might have accepted Carl Weber's help with *Mother Courage* and gone on to introduce more of Brecht's work to Britain. But in this refusal lay her consistency as a human being and her vitality as an artist and teacher.

3
Roger Planchon

Planchon's contribution to directors' theatre is rather different from Joan Littlewood's, though grounded in a comparable vision of theatre for the people. Just as Littlewood remained faithful to Stratford East, so Planchon has refused to move from Villeurbanne, a working-class suburb of Lyon, and has had the satisfaction (denied to Littlewood) of seeing the cultural authorities endorse this stand, transferring the prestigious title 'Théâtre National Populaire' from Paris to Villeurbanne. Both directors consider the political and the artistic problems of theatre directing to be inseparable. Both were able to attract excellent actors and to retain their loyalty for long enough to build up an ensemble. But Planchon has not been a great champion of the collaborative process. Since the 1960s, when he began to write his own plays, he has gradually extended his own control of the creative process, becoming, like Craig's 'stage director', a master of all techniques: he is a powerful actor, a prolific inventor of stage images, a playwright of originality and complexity.

Directing, for him, involves a mobilisation of all these skills in some degree and he has gone so far as to claim that the director's work should be accorded equal status with that of the playwright. He claimed that it too should be seen as a kind of writing – 'scenic writing' – employing the specific language of theatre: movement, sound, gesture, colour, and so on. He was strongly influenced by Brecht in the mid 1950s, developing his notion of scenic writing from a meditation on Brecht's work. Since encountering Robert Wilson in the early 1970s, he has placed even greater emphasis on the directing process as the generation of a rich sequence of complex images. He is fond of comparing theatre with other visual arts, especially painting and cinema.

Planchon's background, like Littlewood's, was simple: his father ran a café in Lyon and his grandfather was a peasant farmer in the Ardèche. He was educated by the friars but rejected both church and school at an early age, taking undemanding jobs while he embarked on a self-devised course of cultural exploration. He attended whatever performances he could afford, recited poetry in literary cafés and jazz clubs, attended short courses in drama. In 1950, still not yet twenty, he grouped together a small company of friends with whom he devised a collage of scenes by Courteline and Labiche under the title *Bottines, collets montés*. The show won them first prize in a competition for regional companies, and with their prize money they decided to turn professional. In Lyon in 1950 there was no tradition of political theatre available, as there had been for Littlewood in Manchester in the 1930s, so the young Théâtre de la Comédie turned instead to popular comedy, mime and music-hall: they developed a rapid-fire burlesque style that borrowed all the old tricks of boulevard comedy, turning the form against itself so as to create skilful parody. At the same time they attempted more exacting work: Marlowe's *Doctor Faustus* and Shakespeare's *Hamlet*, approaching these classics with an eye to contemporary relevance, much as Littlewood was doing at that time. Although he is now known as an outstanding director of Molière, Planchon at first avoided the French classics, discovering a different tradition, not well known in France, going back through Kleist and Büchner to the Elizabethans. In the course of the 1950s, as Michael Kustow has pointed out, 'Planchon formulated a distinctively modern genealogy for the theatre, rooted in the remarkable early 19th century German romantic drama of playwrights like Büchner who were trying to grapple with social-political change and a psychological complexity of which they were newly aware.'[1] The definition of this modern theatre was to blossom in Planchon's relationship with Adamov and his discovery of Brecht.

At first, in his attempts to build a modern repertoire, he turned mostly to authors associated with surrealism: Ghelderode, Ionesco, Adamov, Prévert and Vitrac; the surrealist current was particularly clear in Vitrac's *Victor* and Ionesco's *Amédée*. He was particularly interested in the combination of parodistic style and dream-like image. From the very beginning the basis of Planchon's work was anti-naturalistic: performances were acrobatic, and the few objects used on stage acquired unusual significance. The result was a style of great intensity, very convincing in its individual elements, but constantly confronting reality rather than imitating it, like a surrealist painting.

In 1953 Planchon gave his first première of a contemporary author with *Le Professeur Taranne* and *Le Sens de la marche* by Arthur Adamov. The encounter with Adamov was to be crucial. The two men discovered common enthusiasms: Artaud, Kleist, Büchner, Bataille,

Kafka, Strindberg. Adamov's willingness to entrust his work to a young unknown provincial director aroused interest; the new journal *Théâtre populaire* sent Jean Duvignaud down from Paris to write a review. In it he commented on Planchon's ability to impose a unity of style, investing both objects and actors with a mysterious power that made them seem larger than life. The plays were performed in the tiny 110-seater Théâtre de la Comedie, into which the company had moved at the beginning of 1953. This building, a disused printing works which they had adapted and reconstructed themselves, was to be their home until 1957, when they moved to Villeurbanne. Here they adopted a policy of alternating burlesque musical comedy shows with experimental work, the former on Fridays, Saturdays and Sundays, since the shows were popular with the Lyon audiences and they could be sure of a sell-out, saving the weekdays for more 'difficult' plays. This policy ensured commercial survival for Planchon at a time when the only other producing theatres outside Paris were the five subsidised regional dramatic centres.

1954 was marked by Planchon's first, rather hesitant Brecht production, *The Good Woman of Setzuan*. It coincided with the Berliner Ensemble's first visit to the West with *Mother Courage*, a production which left a large number of French actors, directors and critics dazzled, but which Planchon missed, being busy on his own production. The Ensemble was invited back to Paris the following year and this time Planchon both saw their work and arranged an interview with Brecht to discuss his production of *The Good Woman*. The meeting lasted for five hours and Planchon has often commented on the decisive nature, for him, of this encounter with the German director. In 1977, for example, he summed it up as follows:

Roger Planchon

Brecht was many things: he was a very original director, who was to have a world-wide influence on theatre aesthetics for the next ten or fifteen years; he was an author, a great author; he was also a considerable theoretician. It was his influence that drove me to read the classics. He insisted on the basic importance of understanding the heritage of the past. I realized I had not read the French classics.[2]

It was Brecht's attitude to the problems of directing in general, and of reworking the classics in particular, that impressed Planchon most strongly. From observing Brecht's productions, Planchon developed his notion of scenic writing:

> The lesson of Brecht is to have declared that a performance combines both dramatic writing and scenic writing; but the scenic writing – he was the first to say this and it seems to me to be very important – has an equal responsibility with the dramatic writing. In fact any movement on the stage, the choice of a colour, a set, a costume etc., involves a total responsibility. The scenic writing has a total responsibility in the same way as writing taken on its own: I mean the writing of a novel or a play.[3]

This statement sums up what Planchon attempted to carry out as a director in the decade that followed. In the productions of this period he developed the concept and the techniques of directing as a complete artistic language – scenic writing. With it came a new richness and complexity of production style. Indeed, the exuberant prodigality of Planchon's work has sometimes provoked the criticism that his scenic writing effectively swamps the dramatic writing of the author it was supposed to serve. While some of his recent productions cannot entirely escape this criticism, those of the 1950s and 1960s were disciplined exercises in establishing the specific historical reality demanded by a given playtext. Respect for historical realities was evident in the only two plays by Brecht that Planchon chose to direct after *The Good Woman: Fear and Misery of the Third Reich* (1956) and *Schweyk in the Second World War* (1961). The Brechtian influence was principally apparent, however, in Planchon's productions of the classics, notably *Henry IV* (1957) and his first Molière, *George Dandin* (1958).

The key to both of these productions was the elaboration of a new scenic language that could cut through the familiar 'classic' associations of the plays. Where such associations tended to stress their universal, ahistorical qualities, Planchon aimed for a style that was entirely applicable to today because it respected the particular social realities from which the play had sprung. Brecht had used the word *Historisierung* to convey the use of historical distance in order to establish a contrast between contemporary social realities and those of a different period. Its function was to provoke an audience to recognise its own daily reality with fresh eyes. This did not mean, for Planchon, a return to naturalism or meticulous historical reconstruction. On the contrary, the scenic language that he developed was one which could establish that particular double focus referred to by Brecht, establishing a critical reflection on our own historical period by means of a carefully directed reflection on a different historical period.

Planchon also learned from Brecht a new sense of the importance of narrative in the theatre. Brecht chose the word 'epic' for this theatre in order to emphasise the fact that for him action and situation were more important than character study. Planchon's approach to directing came to focus primarily on the actions of the characters. He would ask not what they *are*, not even what they *say*, but what they *do*. Although this approach became clearest in his productions of Shakespeare and Molière, it was already a feature of two productions of new plays, *Aujourd'hui ou les Coréens* by Michel Vinaver in 1956 and *Paolo Paoli* by Adamov in 1957. For both, the setting took on a new fundamental significance. For Vinaver's play, set during the Korean war, the stage was covered with sand, planted with a forest of rushes and scrub in which the actors crawled and wallowed. The vivid presentation on stage of the concrete realities of life for a French soldier caught up in a conflict he did not understand appeared strikingly novel. In an appreciative review Roland Barthes praised the production for its truthfulness and absence of slogans.

In 1957 Planchon's company received its first invitation to perform in Paris where it visited the Théâtre du Vieux Colombier with *Paolo Paoli*. The production was condemned by the right-wing Jean-Jacques Gautier as an unpatriotic attempt to sully the glorious image of France during the *belle époque*. When left-wing critics leapt to Planchon's support, he acquired a misleading reputation as a left-wing propagandist. His own most urgently felt need at this time was to expand beyond the confines of a small 'art' theatre. Just at this moment came the opportunity to move to the large municipal theatre of Villeurbanne, an adjoining industrial suburb some three miles from the centre of Lyon. The size of the theatre (more than a thousand seats) and its location offered Planchon the chance to emulate Jean Vilar's success at the Théâtre National Populaire in Paris. Vilar had written that theatre must be seen as a public service, just like gas, water or electricity. Planchon decided to see if this conception of theatre could work in the sort of place where it was most needed: a provincial working-class suburb which, without its theatre, would be like any other culturally underprivileged conurbation. The theatre was renamed 'Théâtre de la Cité' to emphasise Planchon's desire to make it into a community theatre, and for his opening productions he distributed a questionnaire among the people of Villeurbanne, offering them a choice of programmes. The two most popular authors to emerge were Shakespeare and Dumas, and so the theatre opened with *Henry IV* followed by an adaptation of *The Three Musketeers*.

Henry IV was generally considered to be a triumph and won Planchon the acceptance of his Villeurbanne audience as well as the approval of the Paris critics. His treatment of the play presented a number of original features. In the first place he rejected the standard translation by François-Victor Hugo. Instead he commissioned a literal translation and then reworked it himself and in rehearsal, until it reached the desired qualities of clarity and dramatic force. His version was faithful to Shakespeare's plot with a minimum of cuts. It was played in two three-hour sections, Part 1 renamed *Le Prince* and Part 2 *Falstaff*. Secondly, Planchon broke with the heroic style of Jean Vilar in *Richard II* and Corneille's *Le Cid*, which had come to be considered as the right way to perform Shakespeare for a popular audience. Vilar's style had assimilated Shakespeare to Corneille, emphasising the study of individual characters and their moral dilemmas. In *Henry IV* Planchon revealed a play of a different kind. As André Gisselbrecht put it, 'here the characters are never treated in isolation, for themselves alone, but always through great historical collisions. Here individual destinies are indissolubly linked with the collective destiny, psychology with politics.'[4] Planchon encouraged his actors to emphasise the discontinuities evident in Shakespeare's characters, not to try for a carefully unified psychological study. The effect of this was to lay stress on the dialectical interplay between the characters and their social conditions.

Together with his stage designer, René Allio, Planchon developed ways of clarifying the complex social stratification present in Shakespeare's play. For the common people rough materials were used with dull colours; the soldiers with no rank wore impersonal costumes with suggestions of leather, metal and stiffness. The lords wore emblems of their riches; their costumes were colourful, obviously fashionable, and suggested warmth. A distinction was established between the holders of political power (Westmoreland, Northumberland) the heads of clans (Percy, Glendower, Mortimer, Hastings) the reliable warriors (Blunt, Mowbray, Warwick) and the younger nobles (Lancaster, Gloucester, Clarence), whose costumes displayed more frivolity or luxury.

The second aim of the production was to do justice to the narrative speed and vigour of Shakespeare's play. The backdrops were enlarged medieval maps, constantly reminding the spectator of the political and territorial struggle at the heart of the plot. Rapid shifts from place to place were achieved by means of models placed on either side of the stage, representing, in emblematic form, London, the Gadshill road, the tavern, the royal palace, and so on. Associated with these models, which were placed to the left or the right of the slightly raised playing area, were a number of key props or items of furniture: for instance, a throne for the palace, stools and a barrel for the tavern. These objects were carefully designed so as to give the impression of being well used and they were thoroughly integrated into the patterns of movement and action.

Contemporary critics were struck most forcefully by the quality of the performances, particularly the ensemble playing. Until recently this was an important element in all of Planchon's production work, despite his increasing tendency to invite star performers from cinema or boulevard theatre to take principal roles. For *Henry IV* and *George Dandin*, he relied solely on the members of his company. Claude Lochy, one of the original group from 1950, composed the music. Allio built the models himself and all the members of the company had a hand in the elaboration of the text. The second quality noted by critics was the 'modernity' of the production. By this they meant that, although the costumes and properties placed the production firmly where Shakespeare set it, at the end of the medieval period, everything about the production encouraged the spectator to judge it with a contemporary eye. Planchon appears to have achieved this by laying stress on the discontinuities in the characters' actions and by pointing up contrasts between words and deeds. André Gisselbrecht cites a scene in which the Archbishop of York vituperates against the fickleness of the people, fed up with the usurper to the point of indigestion: 'as soon as we are shown this feudal lord speaking of indigestion while gulping down cakes served on a silver salver, then his words lose their absolute value and hence their credibility'. In another example, the rebels decided on the partition of England while sharing out a meal round a table. Today such techniques are part of the general heritage of the Brechtian tradition and are all too often misused or overused. But in 1957 in Villeurbanne they had the force of a revelation. The result of his production was to present a vast and detailed reflection on problems of power and its legitimacy, of order versus disorder and of ideas of national unity. As the Algerian war was building towards its crisis, these themes had an obvious relevance to contemporary France and one that was not missed by the spectators. Gisselbrecht summed it up as 'a large lesson in politics conducted with the speed of a Western'. It is clear that, while using techniques borrowed from Brecht (the production also employed screened summaries of each scene before it took place), Planchon had managed to do more than just copy: he had created a form of epic theatre complex enough to delight both Paris critics and local audiences.

Perhaps the most successful application of these production methods to the classics was in *Le Tartuffe* (1962). In this production Planchon's fascination with history led him to construct a scenic language of very considerable complexity. The play was presented against the background of a society undergoing a process of transformation. Planchon gave full weight to the element of contemporary social comment in the play, suggesting the real political balance of forces that existed in France in the 1660s: the young Louis XIV has successfully played off the new bourgeoisie against the feudal nobility, terminating the Fronde (civil war) and founding the modern French state, every aspect of which is rapidly being unified beneath his absolute power. Catholicism supplies both the ideological expression of this unity and an efficient regulator of his subjects' behaviour in both the private and the public aspects of their lives. Proceeding, as before, not from the question 'who are the characters?' but 'what do the characters do?', Planchon found to his surprise that Tartuffe does not behave with the sly hypocrisy which his name summons to mind. On the contrary, he is almost entirely passive. It is Orgon who acts, who insists on the marriage to Mariane, on disinheriting his own son in Tartuffe's favour, who first brings up the subject of Argas's chest of compromising papers, insisting on giving it to Tartuffe. The only times when Tartuffe acts decisively are the times when he betrays himself – that is, when he fails to play the hypocrite successfully: in his seduction of Elmire and his attempt to evict Orgon at the end of the play. This episode became, in Planchon's production, a terrifying demonstration of the all-pervading tentacles of the absolute power of Louis XIV, comparable to that of a Stalin in the twentieth century. If Orgon was saved, at the last minute, from the clutches of Tartuffe, it was only because he had proved useful to the King in the past and might do so again.

René Allio's set consisted of a highly polished floor of different coloured wooden tiles arranged in classical

4a.   *Tartuffe* (1962): Design by René Allio

patterns. This was enclosed by walls made up of paintings from the period, chosen to reinforce the atmosphere of a life bathed in religious devotion. Crucifixions, depositions, martyrdoms, these paintings presented Christs and saints in various stages of undress, with a repeated ambiguity as to whether they were in agony or in ecstasy. Occasional items of richly inlaid wooden furniture helped to increase the suggestion of Versailles: Orgon's house was a small copy of Louis XIV's own ostentatious prosperity. Orgon was portrayed as a man dissatisfied with these comfortable surroundings, fascinated instead by the image of pious austerity which Tartuffe represented for him. Planchon caused considerable scandal in French academic circles by suggesting that Orgon's attraction towards Tartuffe contained an element of unconscious homosexuality. This was considered to be taking contemporary relevance too far. But Planchon was unrepentant: he suggested that the play should be seen both as a bourgeois comedy and as a political thriller. It is bourgeois comedy because it was the first play of its kind in the French repertoire based on adultery. The fact that Orgon's infatuation was not with another woman but with another man (and a man posing as a saint) provided the play with its cruel ambiguity, since in Orgon's blind attraction for Tartuffe emotional and religious feelings become confused. It is a political thriller because its narrative concerns an important member of the upper bourgeoisie who, in the aftermath of a civil war, has maintained contacts with the defeated opposition, and who is nearly ruined by the machinations of a swindler out to feather his own nest.

The play enacts a process of stripping-away, until Tartuffe's real motives are clear and Orgon is disabused. At the end of each act, one of Allio's walls flew up, revealing another behind it until, at the end of the play, the

4b. *Tartuffe* (1962): Roger Planchon (Tartuffe) and Anouc Ferjac (Elmire)

decorative elements in the house had been stripped bare. The performances were, for Planchon's company, rather sober and restrained. There was relatively little movement or additional business, the costumes were rather austere, mostly in dark colours, suggesting more Louis XIII than Louis XIV and there was only a hint of modernity in the boots and coats worn by the bailiffs who came in at the end to take possession of the house. A well-known film actor, Michel Auclair, was brought in to play Tartuffe, a role which Planchon himself took on in subsequent revivals. Far from playing Tartuffe as the usual slimy caricature, Auclair made him seem young, not unattractive and above all very secretive, as befitted a successful swindler trying to play a pious role.

The production was one of the company's major successes and was revived regularly until the Villeurbanne theatre closed for renovations in 1969. In 1973 a new version opened with fresh designs by Hubert Monloup. The new settings retained some of the features of the old, including the principle of gradually stripping the set until harsh, prison-like stone walls were revealed at the end. But the details of both sets, costumes and performances were recast in more physical form. This time the aim was to show a moment of past time which is in the process of demolition and of transformation. The reign of the young Louis is just beginning and old forms are being broken up to create the new Louis XIV style. In each of the successive settings designed by Monloup, there was evidence of builders at work: the social transformation of the mid seventeenth century here found expression in the literal transformation of Orgon's house from Renaissance fortress to showy Louis XIV mansion. Each scene presented juxtapositions of the old and new: for example, the first scene included a life-size statue of Christ as a rather dejected man-of-sorrows seated on a plank, on which the actors would also sit from time to time, turning their back on him. Hanging above was a triumphant angel blowing a trumpet, and the contrast between these two religious images suggested the contrast between the suffering servant whom Tartuffe apes and the Catholic triumphalism that served Louis XIV's purpose in establishing his centralised, totalitarian state.

When Orgon entered (coming home from a journey) the first thing he did was to have his court clothes removed and to put on a loose robe instead. Instead of wearing formal clothes throughout, as they had done in the 1962 production, the actors now put on grand costume only for public occasions. The rest of the time, when the action concerned only members of the family, they wore informal dress – shifts, shirts, robes. This greatly enhanced the audience's awareness of the intimate nature of the family drama (as well as respecting historical accuracy): Tartuffe's penetration into the most secret aspects of the family's life became almost tangible. In the acting style employed for the new production there was much more physical business and movement around the stage. Most strikingly, the ambiguous swooning gestures of the Christs and saints on Allio's walls were incorporated into the gestures and body movements of the actors themselves. This was clearest in Act III, scene iv, where Tartuffe accuses himself before Orgon. Planchon, in the role of the hypocrite, almost literally collapsed in Orgon's arms, so that Orgon had to support him physically as well as emotionally.

Physicality was one of the keys to this production, partly because a central theme of the play is the contrast between appearance and reality. Because Orgon is fooled by Tartuffe's appearance, he can use his real parental authority to force his daughter to marry the hypocrite. The scene in which Mariane begs for mercy stressed how Orgon

5a. *Tartuffe* (1973): Design by Hubert Monloup; Guy
     Tréjean (Orgon), Roger Planchon (Tartuffe)

was physically sacrificing his daughter by presenting
Mariane in a state of semi-hysteria, rushing from one side
of the stage to the other, and requiring three other women
to control her. Similarly, the seduction scene, in which
Orgon is finally convinced of the reality of Tartuffe's
betrayal, was presented in very concrete terms; in her
desperation to alert her husband to what was going on,
Elmire climbed onto the table under which Orgon was
hiding, then rolled off in despair, wrapping the tablecloth
round her like a sheet.

The violence of the last act was also heightened in this
second production. The King's envoy and his men entered
with a considerable show of force. Orgon and his family
were herded into pits suggesting dungeons beneath the
stage floor, while Tartuffe was gagged and his servant

5b. *Tartuffe* (1973): The King's officer (Claude Lochy) taunts Tartuffe

Laurent, who had been a silent spy throughout, was bound, stripped and strung up. Everything in the last scene was cold and frightening, especially the sneering, unpredictable tone in which the King's officer delivered his speech in praise of the monarchy. One felt the presence of a man who was extremely dangerous because he had total power and enjoyed making others sweat. By the end of the play the half-finished designs of the different rooms in Orgon's house, which had been removed one by one, came to represent not just bricks and mortar, but Orgon's whole dream of his new social position. So when, in the last scene, these grandiose decors had all disappeared, and he was helpless in the face of the intruders, the audience understood that what had been laid bare was not merely Orgon's private religious and emotional delusions about Tartuffe: it was also his social delusions about the kind of authority a wealthy bourgeois could enjoy under the new regime of Louis XIV.

Planchon's work on *Le Tartuffe* was perhaps the most successful example of directorial methods he was employing throughout the sixties on a variety of plays, including Racine's *Bérénice* (1966) and two more plays by Shakespeare, *Troilus and Cressida* (1964) and *Richard III* (1966). Concerning *Richard III* he wrote,

I cannot live without Shakespeare . . . in his world I feel completely at ease. . . . I find in his plays the two things that excite me and that seem worthy subjects for the theatre: politics and love. In Shakespeare the social analysis never crushes the individual psychology of the characters while at the same time the characters do not mask the general view of the society that is being described.[5]

By the end of the 1960s, Planchon was widely accepted as the leader of a revolution in directing, one that combined social and political commitment with the development of scenic writing of subtlety and complexity. But he had also come under fire for excessive directorial intervention. The critics of *Théâtre populaire*, once his chief supporter, had criticised the 1961 production of *Schweyk*, complaining that he had gone beyond Brecht: 'Planchon is no longer seeking to situate and explain historically a certain dramaturgical practice; he is substituting one form of writing for another. He is replacing a play, that is a narrative and a meaning, by a symbolic system with multiple meanings.'[6] Planchon countered that the reason why his production had not found favour was that he had reached the end of his 'copying' phase and was no longer respecting the Brechtian orthodoxy:

There can be no such thing as Brechtian dogma, neither critically nor creatively. The history of Brecht productions has only just begun. All the scenic methods that we use today and which are of assistance at the level of *contemporary* understanding of Brecht will gradually be abandoned. Without belief in their disappearance, there can be no acceptance of dialectics. And to believe that Brecht's works, resolutely social and historical as they are, cannot be open to new understandings, is to demonstrate only a superficially 'scientific' attitude. Everything is and remains open. There can be no other orthodoxy. . . .[7]

The inventive and irreverent scenic language being developed by Planchon at this time was not condemned by all critics. Denis Bablet, head of theatre research at the Centre National de la Recherche Scientifique wrote,

Planchon and Allio use a stage on which every element of the play's setting is visible from the beginning. On this stage they narrate for us the story of Schweyk and in the process employ any spectacular element that seems useful. Schweyk directed by Planchon becomes both the performance of Brecht's play and the research for new expressive means, a new stage language breaking away from the accepted practices of contemporary French theatre.[8]

Planchon's first decade at the Théâtre de la Cité had coincided with a major effort by André Malraux, Minister of Culture under de Gaulle, to promote a policy of decentralisation of the arts. In 1963 Malraux conferred the status of *centre dramatique national* on the Villeurbanne company and proposed that Planchon should direct a *maison de la culture* in the region. Planchon, however, resisted, because he was wary of the complex funding and governing arrangements envisaged for *maisons de la culture*. He always insisted that financial control and hence policy decisions must be the responsibility of the artistic director. At the end of the 1960s he was offered the post of director of the Théâtre National Populaire in Paris. When he refused to move his base from Villeurbanne to Paris, the title 'Théâtre National Populaire' was transferred from Paris to his theatre at Villeurbanne with effect from the beginning of 1973. With the title came a massively increased subsidy of 6 million francs, but Planchon retained his financial independence and the company continued to function, legally, as a *société anonyme* (a limited company).

The new status conferred on the company coincided with other renewals. In 1969 the theatre had been closed for extensive renovation work which lasted three years. The stage was enlarged and modernised, while the auditorium was converted to a single rake with an improvement in seating but a reduction in total capacity to 800 seats. In the new theatre Robert Gilbert continued as administrative director but the responsibilities of artistic director were shared by Roger Planchon and Patrice Chéreau. Chéreau was the son of a local painter known to Planchon and whose works had been exhibited at the theatre. He had already made a name as an iconoclastic young director with an intensely visual style – qualities that were to become internationally known with his *Ring* cycle at Bayreuth in the late seventies. In Planchon's own directing work of the seventies, concern for visual qualities also became more important. During the first thirteen years at the Théâtre de la Cité he had relied very considerably on the collaboration of his designer, René Allio.

After the three-year fallow period 1969–72, he began to work with different designers. He had been greatly influenced by Robert Wilson's *Deafman Glance*, which visited France in 1971. This production had encouraged his belief in the importance of scenic writing: 'Wilson proves that it is possible to create a scenic writing entirely independent of spoken text. That constitutes a revolution in theatre. He proves that it is possible to create images in the theatre which are not laughable when compared, say, to painting.'[9] Planchon's directing work after 1972 was to place greater emphasis on the creation of images, often inspired by surrealism. Another influence, which had always been latent in his work, but now came more to the surface, was that of Artaud. As a teenager, Planchon had been deeply affected by Artaud's poetry: 'Artaud revealed to me the horror of the twentieth century. At sixteen, on seeing the vistas which he opened up, I was frozen with terror, I admit it. An immense terror. For years, poems by Artaud would make me tremble.'[10] Even more important than outside influences in Planchon's developing directing style was his own experience as a playwright. Here, too, he found himself working through images. Since his very first production in 1950, Planchon had been scripting burlesque comedy shows; in the 1960s he began writing serious plays, to which he devoted progressively more of his creative energies. In 1980 he summed it up: 'In the day-time, I rehearse, I perform; at night I have to be able to sweat blood over three lines of dialogue. Life flies past and each year increases my fear of betraying the real.'[11] His vision of 'the real' embraced both the historical and political realities of Brecht and the surreal vision of Artaud. The subjects he chose were often people on the brink of madness, as in *Gilles de Rais* (1976), his play about the medieval child murderer. Planchon's Gilles is a man trapped between two worlds, the one in its dying spasms, the other not yet born. The medieval age, dominated by the inextricable combination of Catholic Church and feudal system, is drawing to a close, but has not yet been replaced by the Renaissance. Gilles's murders are partly the expression of a death wish, partly an attempt to break out of his ideological impasse. This dilemma was presented through richly emblematic staging, based on images drawn from medieval manuscripts. The last scene, the execution of Gilles and his companions, burned at the stake, was treated as a dream image. Gilles and his fellows reclined on bright red quilts, while the presiding prelates watched from ladders planted in sockets in the stage.[12]

In the 1970s Planchon also returned to two of the contemporary authors whose work he had staged at the Théâtre de la Comédie: Vinaver and Adamov. In both cases his directorial approach was enormously ambitious: with the Vinaver production, he aimed for a comprehensive statement about the world of international big business; with the Adamov production his aim was to present the whole of the writer's life and his relationship with the century in which he lived. Vinaver had written almost nothing for most of the sixties, when he was working as executive director for a large multinational corporation. But at the end of the decade he wrote *Par-dessus bord*, a fabulously inventive play drawing on every major theatre tradition from Aristophanes to 'happenings', and depicting the profound alteration of European business structures under the impact of aggressive American marketing methods. In a highly complex and original dramatic form it goes some way towards meeting Brecht's demand for a play of sufficient scope to show how a decision taken in a Chicago boardroom might affect a peasant living in Ireland. Planchon felt that here was a unique opportunity to present a production dealing with the down-to-earth reality of most people's working lives, but that Vinaver's discontinuous structure, with its overlapping time-scales, actions and places, would be impossible to stage. Consequently he persuaded Vinaver to cut and rewrite the play with a single narrative thread and he added music and dance. Although Vinaver agreed to the changes, he later felt that this had been a mistake and that the result had turned out too much like one of Planchon's own burlesque extravaganzas. It seems that here was an example of Planchon's insistence on narrative leading him into a directorial error which he himself has criticised elsewhere: failure to trust the author's text.

With Adamov, the process was a different one. Here he put together fragments from a number of Adamov's plays in order to create a composite image of the author; the production was entitled *A. A. Théâtres d'Adamov*. Planchon was particularly fascinated by Adamov's rejection of his own early work in the middle fifties, when he first underwent the influence of Brecht. He also responded to Adamov's unusual neurotic obsessions, which were all more or less clearly induced by the pressure of guilt generated in the classic family relationships: father–son, mother–son, and so on. The first part of the production was played in the foyer and consisted of snatches from Adamov's early plays performed very simply in a re-creation of the style of their original productions. While this was going on, the audience (all standing or milling about in the foyer) were surprised to see Laurent Terzieff, in the role of Adamov, break in to criticise and denounce his own work, using the words of Adamov's preface to his second volume of collected plays.

For the second half, the audience moved into the auditorium proper, where they were confronted by a high fence, marked 'PRIVATE PROPERTY', running around an enormous pile of phosphorescent blue sand planted with miniature oil derricks. To one side was a shining chromium railway line running into another dune of sand rising up behind. On that and behind it was a real railway line on which a real revolutionary train rolled in and out at certain points in the action. In this setting, evoking both the easy childhood of Adamov and the treacherous difficulties of acting on shifting sand, as well as the demands of larger social movements breaking in from outside, was played out the story of Adamov's own internal divisions.

Terzieff represented Adamov, the central character in his own plays, placed in a series of situations: the home, the army, the church, the school, in which he repeatedly came up against the authority of a father-figure, always the same. A group of friends who have decided to form a revolutionary party break in at various points and urge him to join them, but he is unable to do so and ends up betraying one of them. In directing this play, Planchon produced some of his most successful effects of visual juxtaposition. For example, taking his cue perhaps from Adamov's autobiography, *L'Homme et l'enfant*, he would include both man and child in the same scene. A case in point was a scene showing the mother desperately asking Terzieff where her little boy is; he becomes very irritated, tells her he hasn't seen the boy, while at the back of the stage, bathed in a weird dream-light, the young Adamov appears with an enormous pistol, which he shoots at the mother before disappearing. The production was filled with such images, possessing precision and clarity but also the hallucinatory quality of a surrealist painting. Adamov had dreamed of a theatre situated at the point where real, material conditions intersect with dreams and neuroses. In this production Planchon succeeded in

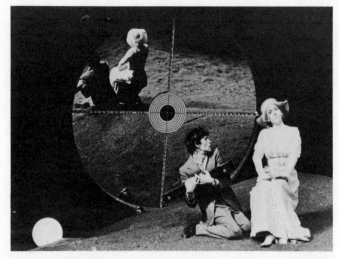

6. *AA Théâtres d'Adamov* (1975): Design by Patrick
    Dutertre and Paul Hanaux; Adamov (Laurent
    Terzieff) confronts the Mother (Pascale de Boysson)

representing the life of a man who had lived at that point
of intersection.

Planchon's mastery of what may be loosely called a
surrealist directing style in the seventies was again apparent
in his first and only production of a contemporary English
dramatist: Pinter's *No Man's Land* (1979). Like the
Adamov production, like Dubillard's *Où boivent les
vaches*, which he directed in 1983, this play concerns a
writer and his relation both to his world of private
obsession and to his own past. Pinter wrote *No Man's Land*
after he had been working on the screenplay for L. P.
Hartley's *The Go-between*, which opens with the phrase
'The past is another country'. In Pinter's play the past
becomes a no man's land which none of the characters can

finally possess, with the result that the present, too, becomes a place of alienation. This central theme was brilliantly illuminated by Planchon's production, which did away with the usual naturalist clutter familiar in English productions of Pinter's work. Instead the action all took place in a strange, bare room furnished only with three black armchairs. The floor was made up of luminous plastic segments coloured blue and white, which gave the audience a strange sensation of floating in space, not unlike that induced by a Magritte painting. The two central roles had been played in England by John Gielgud and Ralph Richardson. Planchon cast two equally famous French actors, Michel Bouquet and Guy Tréjean, who gave performances of great intensity and controlled violence. At the end of the play the whole box set rose very slowly into the air, accompanied by a strangely disturbing noise, at first impossible to identify, but then apparent as thousands of empty bottles, which had been piled behind the backstage walls of the set, were released, crashing onto the floor of the stage and leaving the audience with a final image of an empty alcoholic wasteland.

The design for this production was by Ezio Frigerio, who also collaborated with Planchon on his other major success of this period, the linked productions of Racine's *Athalie* and Molière's *Dom Juan* (1980). These brought together Planchon's preoccupations with love, politics and death, and with the powers of ideology, superstition and belief, expressing these themes through a scenic language of a rare richness and profusion. *Athalie* is a play seldom performed in France; ostensibly about the just purposes of God in history, it derives its power from its very Jansenist presentation of a God whose purposes can never be fully known or understood but who demands blind faith and total obedience.

The drama of the play is provided by a power-struggle between Joad and Athalie. Joad is usually pictured as a worthy Hebrew patriarch, Athalie as a dignified if anguished queen. Planchon's performance as Joad made one think more of an Islamic mullah than of Moses. He was a man illuminated by faith. He spoke rapidly, with laughter in his voice and a characteristic confidence that God was on his side. Athalie also emerged rejuvenated: she was presented as a reasonable, pragmatic politician. Her every action had been taken for the good of the kingdom; her goal had been stability and tolerance. But such worthy aims did not have the force to withstand the determination and fanaticism of Joad. The play interested Planchon, he said, as a commentary on the totalitarian ideology of the age of Louis XIV. Not content with having established absolute

7a.   *Athalie* (1980): Design by Ezio Frigerio; the Angel (Christian Rist) celebrates the triumph of faith over force

control in secular terms, Louis's ambition was to govern the private morality and even the spiritual life of his subjects. The production was rich in images of Catholic triumphalism, the cross and the cannon not so much opposed as mutually reinforcing. Planchon encouraged the audience to reflect along these lines by introducing a tall male angel, dressed in shining golden armour, resembling the young Louis dressed as Apollo for a court ballet.

Athalie and *Dom Juan* were performed on alternate evenings using the same cast and certain elements of the same set (the cupola, for example, was used in both productions). There were some interesting combinations of roles. For example, Gérard Desarthe, who played the role of Mathan in *Athalie*, was cast as Dom Juan – in both plays he presented a challenge to the dominant religious ideology. Similarly, the two peasant girls exploited by Dom Juan were both members of the chorus of terrified girls in *Athalie*. By such means, Planchon presented the two plays as two sides of the same coin: where *Athalie* conveyed the triumph of a totalitarian Catholic ideology (all the stronger for winning against the odds), *Dom Juan* expressed the spirit of dissidence that insists on questioning everything (even at the cost of life itself). The Don's challenge to authority was enacted in a stage setting where everything threatened to overwhelm him: from the violence of the chivalric code, presented in the scene in the forest, to the monstrous death's head of the Commander's tomb; from the pathos of Dona Elvire's appeals, to the very elements themselves – the monumental waves on the seashore, frozen in a movement that seemed to engulf him.

For both plays the set included a short platform, projecting into the auditorium, that was shaped like a black marble tomb watched over by a skeleton. This ever-present reminder of death provided a scenic echo to the constant

7b. *Dom Juan* (1980): Design by Ezio Frigerio; Dom
Juan (Gérard Desarthe) seducing Charlotte (Cathy
Bodet) and Mathurine (Dominique Messali)

warning, in the texts of both plays, of impending doom and
destruction. For both Athalie and Dom Juan are characters
who dream about their own deaths. Both attempt to make a
stand on the set of values they have chosen, but both are
haunted and ultimately destroyed by the power of God.
The experience of seeing these productions was a
particularly satisfying and complex one, because, in
addition to their ideological and social aspects, they
projected a powerful psychological portrait of individuals
attempting to face up to the ultimate question of death. In
the main characters of both productions we were shown
people who were not just constrained by external pressures
but who experienced these pressures as interior
psychological and spiritual struggles.

Roger Planchon

Consistent with his new view of the director's role as that of presenting the evaluation of a writer who must come to grips with both the powers of his own sub-conscious mind and the established powers of his society, Planchon has directed several other composite productions. They include *Folies bourgeoises* (1975), which juxtaposed extracts from the boulevard successes of the last theatrical season before the outbreak of the First World War, and *Ionesco* (1983). But his major project of the early eighties was a Molière film. Cinema producers had regularly asked him for permission to film his productions, but he had always refused, arguing that one of the specific glories of theatre is to be ephemeral. But he proposed instead a composite production based on four of Moliére's early farces: *La Jalousie du Barbouillé*, *Le Mariage forcé*, *Les Précieuses ridicules* and *Monsieur de Pourceaugnac*. Through these texts he saw Moliére, the aging director–playwright and master of his own trade, longing for power of a more tangible nature and obsessed by disturbing erotic desires for young girls who were the same age as his own children. After three years' work on this project, and because of a change in the Gaumont management, Planchon found that he was not allowed to complete the film. Some of the same ideas were used as the basis for his 1986 production of *L'Avare*.

At a time when most of the major European theatres survive largely on a repertoire of revivals of the classics, Planchon is resigned to his role as a kind of museum curator. But he is wary of the fashion for 'rediscovering' classic authors in a new light, a fashion which he himself helped to start in the 1950s. If it is true, as he argued in his preface to *L'Avare*, that each new period 'reads' the works of the past differently and reveals itself through its 'reading', then the work of the director must be to call attention to this process of reading and to the manner in which it is constructed. In doing so, the director will be speaking of the modern world as much as of a distant historical period. In 1977 Planchon enumerated four qualities he claimed were necessary for a director: (1) scenic inventiveness, (2) a feeling for three-dimensional images, (3) the ability to direct actors, and (4) a world-view. His work in the theatre has shown the interdependence of these four aspects, none of which can be satisfactory in isolation. He has become famous for his inventiveness and creation of startling new images; he has also made a major contribution towards the development of the role of the director by defining a new 'scenic language'. In this language, sets, costumes and props are all fully exploited as active bearers of meaning, never simply background for the actors' performances, and they are carefully chosen so as to communicate at both the psychological and social levels. Equally important in his directorial method are the performances he can draw from actors. He has said that his greatest pleasure, as a director, is working with actors on a text, and his own talents as a performer have made him a director with whom actors want to work. When directing actors, he avoids all ready-made approaches, varying his method from performer to performer and from play to play. Rather than a particular training or method, the quality he looks for in an actor is intelligence, and he defines his preferred acting style as light, humorous and 'absolutely stripped bare of pathos'. He admired the relaxed quality of Scofield's performance in Brook's *King Lear*.

The fourth quality, 'a world-view', is more difficult to sum up, but it finds expression in his lifelong commitment to presenting outstanding theatre work in Villeurbanne. His is not a naïve belief that theatre can change society, but a dogged insistence that the best must be made available to those outside the orthodox cultural networks:

> What the great authors speak of concerns people who are outside culture. What Shakespeare speaks of is directed at my mother, who could not read. All are not able to receive it but it is for them. It is for them, ultimately, that the great authors suffer, labour, commit themselves totally. . . . When Artaud said that he wrote for 'the great public of hairdressers' boys, laundry maids, tobacconists, ironmongers, joiners, printing workers', he was telling the truth.[13]

Planchon's attitude to directing is evident in the priority he ascribes to scenic inventiveness and the feeling for three-dimensional images. But, although he admired Robert Wilson's creation of 'a scenic writing entirely independent of spoken text', he has not attempted to copy him. Instead, he has sought to exploit both text and image in the expression of a totality – the whole outlook and life of a given writer in *Ionesco* or *A. A.*; the whole outlook of a given epoch in *Athalie* and *Dom Juan*. He has been criticised for manipulating the work of other authors to suit his own purposes. On occasions, this criticism has certainly been justified; *Par-dessus bord* is a case in point. But often critics have been too misled by Planchon's bold redefinition of a play's visual field to see that the text itself was perfectly respected. In fact, the quality that makes Planchon's work so interesting is his respect for *both* text *and* scenic image. This could be expressed differently by saying that he is both a writer and a director. His directing work is influenced by his concerns as a playwright and *vice versa*. He sees the two activities as separate but complementary. His distinction in both fields makes him unique among contemporary directors.

4
Ariane Mnouchkine

Ariane Mnouchkine first became widely known in the years after 1968 as the director of the Théâtre du Soleil, a model of collaborative organisation. Her company has retained its reputation into the late eighties, although she is almost the sole surviving member from before 1968. Her work is as central to the Théâtre du Soleil as Littlewood's was to Theatre Workshop. Like Littlewood and Planchon, her initial motivation was political as much as artistic, something that is evident in her continued insistence on equality of salaries within the company. Her major contribution to directors' theatre has been to demonstrate the paradox that the greatest directors are not just those who develop a new stage idiom (though she has done this), but those who best succeed in bringing out the talents of their actors. Like Joan Littlewood, she has decried the all-powerful director, yet has not always resisted the temptation to be dictatorial. Her great distinction is to have developed much further than Littlewood ever did the research into popular acting styles, masks, clowning and acrobatics.

Ariane Mnouchkine

Mnouchkine was born in 1939, the daughter of an English actress and a French film producer of Russian descent. Her first theatre work was with university groups at Oxford and at the Sorbonne in Paris, where she founded a student company in 1959. Her activities were cut short when she abandoned her studies in psychology to travel in the Far East. There she discovered at first hand the Indian and Japanese theatre forms that were to influence her later work. Returning to France, she regrouped the student theatre company to form the Théâtre du Soleil. In many ways the company's style and orientation at first differed little from that of many new companies appearing in France in the mid 1960s. They shared a left-wing ideology, an interest in performing for new popular audiences and the concern to discover a new repertoire that would be suitable for such performances. The first two productions of the Théâtre du Soleil were Adamov's adaptation of *The Petits Bourgeois* by Gorki and *Captain Fracasse*, adapted from Gautier's novel by Philippe Léotard, a member of the company. The name 'Théâtre du Soleil' (Theatre of the Sun) was picked by Mnouchkine 'as a tribute to certain film makers associated with light, generosity and pleasure such as Max Ophuls, Jean Renoir, George Cukor',[1] and in this choice can be seen an element of utopianism, even of sentimentality, that was to become a strong distinguishing feature of Mnouchkine's work.

For the company's next production, Mnouchkine proposed *The Kitchen* by Arnold Wesker, whose work had not yet been performed in France. Under her direction, the play, in an adaptation by Léotard, became very different from the wordy original, with its lapses into static set speeches. The first unusual thing about the production was its location: the disused Medrano circus building in Montmartre, due for demolition. The ring was turned into an arena stage, with the audience seated around it in a semi-circle. This setting imposed an ebullient, physical performance style, achieving its effects by patterns of orchestrated movement. The set did not attempt to re-create a realistic kitchen: it left much of the space open with, at the centre, a block of commercial ovens and sinks. Wesker's own suggestion for staging was adopted: 'the waitresses will carry empty dishes, and the cooks will mime their cooking', Mnouchkine had decided that work on mime was essential to develop her company's expressive powers. As the other members of the company still had to go out and work during the day for their living, she followed a course at Lecoq's mime school, passing on what she had learnt when the company met in the evenings. All members spent time observing the work routine in a restaurant kitchen, then worked at a theatrical

8.   *The Kitchen* (1967): Mime used to convey the rhythm of work

transposition of the realities they had observed, so that, by means of mimed gesture and heightened movement, they could present on stage an image of the frantic rhythm and growing tensions of kitchen work. The result was a powerful theatrical metaphor for a working life of any kind.

This production enjoyed a considerable success, which enabled most of the company to turn professional. Mnouchkine now embarked on her first Shakespeare: *A Midsummer Night's Dream* (1968), French version again by Léotard. This production showed her increasing interest in the use of expressive movement on stage, the roles of Oberon and Titania being given to dancers from Maurice Béjart's contemporary ballet company. This play too was performed in the Medrano circus. This time half of the raised portion, as well as the ring, was used for the action, and the whole arena was covered in animal skins. The production stressed the violent, elemental qualities of the play, with the fairies played as dangerous, satyr-like creatures, dressed in goatskin trousers, their chests daubed in blood. Oberon and Titania were dressed in light silks and moved with airy, gliding motions across the vast open space. The comic scenes with the lovers anticipated some of the freedom and vigour of Brook's production two years later. The least successful part of Mnouchkine's production was the depiction of the mechanicals. For Brook, the seriousness of the mechanicals' efforts provided an essential contrast with the fundamental frivolity or irresponsibility of both lovers and fairies. In this way, though comic, they acquired a certain dignity and power of their own, despite their lack of both artistic ability and social rank. Mnouchkine interpreted the mechanicals as naïve clowns, dressed them in silly costumes and encouraged them to play the parts for knockabout humour. This was largely unsuccessful and the performance concluded by eradicating all social differences as the mechanicals, fairies, lovers and aristocrats all joined hands for an immense round dance.

The political upheavals of May 1968 caused turmoil among left-wing theatre workers in France. With demonstrations in the streets and occupations in the factories, theatre appeared to have come into its own as a medium of popular expression. Interrupting its Shakespeare run, the Théâtre du Soleil went into occupied factories to perform *The Kitchen* and to discuss the problems of how to re-create the traditions of popular theatre. The immediate result of these experiences was a reorganisation of the company (already legally established as a co-operative) to ensure absolute equality of salaries and a minimum of division of the work into specialised jobs. An equally important change was the group's decision to abandon work on playtexts, constructing shows instead from their own creative resources. The first of these was *The Clowns* in 1969. In their search for a more popular performance idiom, Mnouchkine suggested that they work not on story or character but on mask. Prompted by their experience of performing in a circus, they decided that each actor would copy the persona of a particular clown, then work on sketches that would show the social function of that clown. The final show was a series of group improvisations and solo 'turns', with the addition of music, songs and gags.

This work on *The Clowns* was decisive for Mnouchkine's development as a director, opening up the possibilities of a group creative process to which each member of the company could contribute, building up a complete performance by means of improvisation. Her role was to stimulate, then to control and shape, these improvisations. This working method is what distinguishes Mnouchkine

from most other directors; she has continued to develop
and refine it over the past two decades, though it has been
modified in order to be applicable to playtexts by
Shakespeare, Cixous and Mnouchkine herself.

In 1970, after *The Clowns*, the company wanted to devise
a play dealing with contemporary political reality. With the
return to power of a conservative government, the most
important question for the members of the Théâtre du
Soleil was: why did the near-revolution of 1968 fail? To
answer this, they first tried working on the Paris Commune
of 1871 and then turned instead to the French Revolution.
Here, they felt, was a subject which was part of common
mythology, yet one which was universally misunderstood.
For Mnouchkine, the Revolution was not a mindless
bloodbath, but the first great popular movement of revolt
against social injustice. As such, it contained the seeds of
an ideal society: a phrase from St Just became the subtitle
of the play: 'Revolution should only stop at the perfection
of happiness.' But she also considered that the positive
aspects of the Revolution had been 'confiscated', since the
aristocracy of the nobles, when overthrown, was quickly
replaced by the new aristocracy of the rich, and so the
French Revolution marked the appearance of capitalism.

The working methods employed in the preparation of
1789 were quite new for the company. The first necessity
was to get to know the historical period in great detail; the
task of research and documentation was divided up among
different members of the group and the results pooled.
They consulted historical works, attended special lectures
and screenings and then used the material acquired for
improvisation work. What emerged, under Mnouchkine's
guidance, was not a single account of the events of the
Revolution, but a collage of sketches representing many
different viewpoints, often the same event as viewed by

different characters or classes. An example near the beginning was the scene of the *cahier des doléances* (list of grievances), which began with the reciting of an edict promulgated by Louis XVI in 1789. In this, the King complained of disturbances in the realm and invited any subject who felt he had a grievance to write to him explaining the nature of that grievance. As he read out this edict, Louis was surrounded, in a carefully constructed image, by idealised shepherdesses who leaned their heads on his lap or his shoulder in attitudes of trustfulness. This was immediately followed by a scene in which a peasant family was shown reacting joyfully to the news of the King's invitation. They resolved in their enthusiasm to write to him, but were immediately faced with the problem of materials: a feather was plucked from a chicken (mimed) to use as a quill; a sheet was torn up to serve as paper; even the

9. *1789* (1970): Louis XVI (M. Godard) as Good Shepherd

lack of ink was overcome by the peasant cutting his own vein to use blood. Only then do they (and the audience) realise that they have never been taught how to write: the myth of feudal paternalism has been exposed. Not only events, but individual characters too, were represented in alternative guises. Louis XVI, for example, was portrayed by a number of different actors in the course of the play, some more sympathetically than others. This process was pushed to further extremes when Louis was played by a puppet: an episode representing the convocation of the three estates was performed satirically by hand puppets; a later episode showing the women of Paris bringing the King back from Versailles presented him as a gigantic carnival figure carried in triumph over the heads of the crowd.

The effect of this variety of representational methods was to oblige the audience to think not just about the events themselves but also about the historical problem of how we relate to these events, picture them and understand them. This might have given rise to an excessively cerebral production, but Mnouchkine avoided this danger by constantly varying the scenic methods and emphasising the self-consciously theatrical devices being used. Certain scenes aimed to provoke a gut reaction: in one, the audience saw a peasant woman flanked by a nobleman and a prelate, each demanding his tax or tithe. Getting no response, they seized the only thing she had, a cooking pot, which broke in half, and the scene ended on her screams of anguish, helplessness and revolt. Contrasting with this straightforward depiction of poverty and oppression was a scene entitled 'The King's Betrayal', in which the power of court intrigue to affect the king's judgement was suggested by portraying Cagliostro as a magician, who whipped up Marie-Antoinette and her ladies into a wild dervish dance. Here the dance of possession worked, not as a literal

10.   *1789*: Court ladies stirred up by Cagliostro

picture of how court ladies behaved, but as a metaphorical representation of court intrigue, its methods and consequences.

The play closed with a speech by Gracchus Babeuf, read out by one of the actors, in which he declared that the oppression of the poor by the rich effectively constituted a state of civil war which could only be resolved by the overthrow of all existing institutions. This naturally opened the way for discussions between actors and audience, which invariably followed performances of this play. Audiences felt all the more inclined to stay and talk because of the unusual spatial arrangement of the performance, which was Mnouchkine's major stroke of directorial genius. The performance was given on not one but five stages, linked by runways surrounding the spectators, who were thus obliged to keep on the move. Some scenes took place on one stage only; some were simultaneously duplicated on two or more stages, moved around the area or came down into the audience. Because of this, audiences experienced a close sense of involvement in the action which tended to engage their emotions at the expense of the critical, thought-provoking elements mentioned above. The climax of this process was the scene of the taking of the Bastille, for which each actor positioned himself at a different point in the central area, gathering a small knot of spectators around him and describing the storming of the prison as if he was telling it to a few friends. As the account built to an exciting climax, spectators became aware that all the others were sharing the same experience until their sense of identity with the revolutionary mass was completed by the explosion of popular festivity, accompanied by music, dancing, wrestling and acrobatics.

Mnouchkine required a large open space for this style of production. This time she found it in the hangars of a disused cartridge warehouse at Vincennes, today known simply as the Cartoucherie. For *1789* she only had time to prepare one of these hangars, but soon the company had expanded into three, and the unusual nature of this performance space has played a vital role in each of Mnouchkine's subsequent productions. Each hangar measures some 20 by 40 metres. The first acts as a reception area, with a bar. The actors take turns to serve and clean up, maintaining the principle that all should share, even in menial tasks. The bar offers rough red wine or beer for sale, together with sandwiches of coarse peasant bread. The second and third hangars are used for performance, including preparation, warming-up, costuming and making-up, all of which take place in an unscreened area open to scrutiny by spectators before they take their places. Mnouchkine herself is much in evidence, seeing to last-minute preparations. She claims that this openness is essential for establishing the right relationship with the audience: one in which the actors do not seek to dazzle, but invite participation, an invitation enthusiastically received by audiences for *1789*. The play's novel actor–audience relationship, its vigour, excitement and fierce commitment to social justice, touched a deep chord in its predominantly youthful spectators, many of whom felt betrayed by the events of 1968. Here they experienced renewed hope, and celebrated a near-religious belief in utopia. The celebratory aspects of the performance were so powerful that the enraptured audiences almost seemed to overlook the critical aspects of the show; in the heady enjoyment of liberty, equality and fraternity, those parts of the play which stressed the failure of the Revolution lost much of their force.

The audiences which flocked to the Cartoucherie in the early 1970s came to share in a privileged moment of joy and festivity which they knew they would find nowhere else. This exceptional emotional force was one consequence of the unity of purpose Mnouchkine had succeeded in establishing within the company. This was expressed by the actors in interviews given at the time of *1789* in phrases such as 'here I am in profound personal agreement with what I perform professionally . . . all work is undertaken entirely in common . . . the Théâtre du Soleil is a way of life for this group, in total harmony with what it is accomplishing'. Mnouchkine agreed: 'Through our work we experience a profound harmony amongst ourselves which extends beyond the ending of the performance'.[2] This sense of a whole community with shared aims and methods was even more important for *1793*, in which the life of a whole *section* of *sans culottes* during 1792–3 was re-created. Work on this play began with a suggestion from Mnouchkine that each actor should develop storytelling skills. Once again, historical research was undertaken, but this time the results were presented in the form of accounts given by one member of the *section* to another. For example, the machinations of the Girondin faction were recounted by a servant in a Girondin household. There was no 'casting' as such; Mnouchkine simply encouraged each actor to develop a character of his own choosing, with a trade, a background, appropriate voice, movements, costume, habits. Because of the narrow social focus, by comparison with *1789*, there was much more attention to concrete historical detail. Nevertheless, Mnouchkine warned the actors against Stanislavskian realism, or the illusionistic re-creation of an historical character; instead she worked, as always, for a distanced performing style which placed emphasis not on the 'flesh and blood reality' of the characters so much as on the political choices they had to face and their gradual development of a useful vocabulary and style of discourse. One of her directorial methods was to work with the women on chorus scenes from Greek tragedy, helping to develop a kind of group voice. With its careful historical setting, its emphasis on narrative, on distanced acting, and on the common people finding their own voice, this was the most Brechtian of Mnouchkine's productions.

It was followed by *L'Age d'or*, the last of the company's group creations. The title was intended to be ambiguous, suggesting both the 'golden age' of legend or of utopian longing, and the discrepancies between that and the present age of capitalist conflict, in which gold, or money, counts for everything. Once again, Mnouchkine's main concern was with discovering the correct performance style. When new ideas were slow in coming, she insisted on a return to first principles, working once again on clowns, masks and *commedia* scenarios. When challenged to

11. *1793* (1972): The women of the section shred lint for
     the hospital

explain the unity of her work, she said it consisted in the
search for a language or form, citing both Copeau and
Meyerhold:

> [Copeau wrote] 'we must destroy existing forms and
> return to primitive forms, such as that of the fixed
> character' . . . to which Meyerhold replied without
> knowing, 'This is why our actors long to dive into the
> study of the fabulous techniques of earlier epochs when
> theatre was theatrical'[3]

The play adopted fixed characters similar to those of the
commedia and presented images of contemporary France
from the point of view of Abdallah, an immigrant worker
arriving in Marseilles from Morocco. Abdallah's
experiences provided a loose narrative thread on which to

hang a picture of modern France from the point of view of the dispossessed who have nothing to sell but their labour. At the end Abdallah fell from scaffolding and was killed, which at last provoked his oppressed fellows to round on their exploiters. This ending was a piece of sheer wish-fulfilment, contradicting everything that had gone before, and Mnouchkine expressed a sense of despair at the difficulties of developing a form effective at both political and theatrical levels.[4] Once again, the play's main success was in creating moments of festivity. The *Cartoucherie* space was transformed by piling tons of earth into dunes, covered with hessian matting. The audience sat on these slopes, moving from space to space as invited by the performers. No other scenic elements were used (apart from a remarkable lighting design, building on a similar success in *1793*) and the challenge for the actors was to bring a whole world to life using only their own physical resources, with no barrier between themselves and the audience.

L'Age d'or took a year of improvisation to prepare and even then was subtitled 'first version'. No subsequent version followed, and, indeed, the struggle to achieve even this much seems to have put intolerable strains on the will of the company members to work together in this way. It was effectively their last collaborative effort, although many of them took parts in Mnouchkine's next project, a film of the life of Molière and his company. This was followed, in 1979, by a play which Mnouchkine herself adapted from Klaus Mann's novel *Mephisto*. In both of these she developed a self-reflective meditation on the function of theatre in society; both works suggested that within a theatre company it is possible to establish a microcosm of democratic practice, but that harmonious community was not strong enough to resist political pressures from outside, nor to exert an influence on political life at large.[5] These pessimistic conclusions certainly reflected Mnouchkine's own experience of finding herself driven farther and farther from her stated aim of reducing the power of the director and relying solely on the creativity of a company of actors. The strains of producing *L'Age d'or* had led to the departure of almost all the older members of the company, such as Jean-Claude Penchenat, who established his own Théâtre du Campagnol in 1976. For both the Molière film and *Mephisto*, Mnouchkine had found it necessary to assume total authority as both writer and director.

It no longer seemed possible to return to the methods of collective creation. After struggling for a while with an original play on recent political events in South East Asia, Mnouchkine found that she could make no progress, so decided to turn back to Shakespeare. She recruited a large number of young people to the company and announced a cycle of six plays: *Richard II*, the two parts of *Henry IV*, *Henry V*, *Twelfth Night* and *Love's Labour's Lost*. In the programme to *Richard II* she wrote, 'we embark on this cycle as one enters an apprenticeship in the workshop of a master craftsman, hoping to learn how to represent the world in a theatre'. Shakespeare was chosen, she said, as someone who had succeeded in writing plays of a historical and political nature without the constraints of realistic psychology; in his plays she discovered a form of expression purely of the theatre and quite specific to it. She began to think about the plays not in terms of individual character study, but in images of a whole social structure, steeped in ritual, and Shakespeare's world suddenly seemed very similar to medieval Japan. The oriental theatre forms which she had studied in the early 1960s rely on the presentation of character defined by movement and gesture, costume and mask, rather than by realistic psychological detail. The strength of such an approach, as Mnouchkine's earlier work showed is that it frees the actors from expending their energies on conjuring up an illusion and enables them instead to act as commentators. The weakness of this approach is that it favours the emergence of types or fixed characters: the hero, the wastrel, the clown, and so forth. This may be appropriate when dealing with mythical material, but applied to contemporary history it can result in drastic over-simplification as later proved to be the case with *Norodom Sihanouk*.

Everything Mnouchkine has said about her approach to Shakespeare concerns this problem of finding appropriate images, sounds and performance style. She has never discussed Shakespeare's own philosophy or interpretation of history, which seems odd in view of her avowed desire to learn how to write a history play. She has even gone so far as to state that Shakespeare's greatness can be attributed to his ideological neutrality. Her interpretation of the plays was thus grounded in an attempt to represent the action in a mythical, timeless light, not to establish any obvious relevance for today. In rehearsals she stressed that Shakespeare's characters had an element of divinity: 'for *Richard II* we decided the characters were men–gods', a very exaggerated interpretation of the doctrine of the divine right of kings. She approached the events of *Richard II* neither as the political story of a power-struggle, nor as the psychological study of a man coming to terms with kingship and its loss, but as a ritual having a special 'relationship with the sacred'. The exact nature of 'the sacred' and precise function of the ritual were left undefined; no attempt was made to allude to the vigorous Reformation spirit which characterised Shakespeare's age. The links with the sacred were limited to Richard's insistence on his divine right and Bolingbroke's desperate desire to appropriate this right. Director and actors had to cast around for adequate images of ritualised power which would not appear stale or weakened by over-use. The predominantly Japanese style answered this need partly because of its essentially alien quality, partly because it was rich in external gesture of an unfamiliar kind. Mnouchkine was deliberately searching for a stage language which could convey distance: 'Shakespeare is not our contemporary and must not be treated as such. He is distant from us, as distant as our own profoundest depths.'[6]

In early rehearsal work, the actors were masked, obliging them to rely on mime and movement. Each actor was encouraged by Mnouchkine to express, physically, a basic emotional state, which she named an *état*, conveying his approach to the world and to the other characters. This word *état* was used to indicate the primary passion which inhabits the actor. Through this primary *état*, a number of secondary emotions could be demonstrated; their external manifestation would vary according to that character's primary *état*. Thus two different characters would find quite different gestures to convey the same emotion. Success or failure in portraying a character was judged not by the usual criteria of realism but, quite differently, by the actor's inventiveness in externalising emotional states. The process recalls the biomechanics of Meyerhold, to whom Mnouchkine made frequent reference. Like the Russian director, she insisted that when an actor portrays a character who is angry he must draw a physical outline of that anger, he must 'put it into actions'. Final casting was left as late as possible and parts seem to have gone to those actors who managed to impose their vision of the character on the rest of the company. Philippe Hottier (the gardener, Sir Toby Belch, Falstaff) described the pressures of this working method as 'a sort of permanently competitive improvisation on the text, where the actor necessarily finds himself competing, in front of Ariane, both against himself and against the others, urged to do better than himself and to do better than them'.[7]

The production's major innovation was in its use of live music, developed by Jean-Jacques Lemêtre in the course of the rehearsals. Lemêtre, a versatile composer and performer, developed an original musical idiom, borrowing from both Eastern and Western sources and relying chiefly on a vast range of percussion instruments. A characteristic sound or sequence of sounds became associated with each character or episode, this musical commentary accompanying every word and action of the play. This had its influence on the actors' delivery of their words: natural inflexions and modulations of the voice were avoided and the words were hammered out in declamatory fashion. The costumes, like the music, were a mixture of oriental and Western elements.

The music, the costumes and the acrobatic vigour of Mnouchkine's young company all combined to effect in the dazzling entrances and exits, made along runways leading off the stage at right-angles. The stage itself was bare and very large (about 18×18 metres). Each entrance was preceded by loud percussion, then the actors ran at breakneck speed, leaping and capering as if on horseback, wheeling around the whole expanse of the stage before taking up position. Throughout many scenes they continued to flex their knees, stamp their feet and manipulate imaginary reins, so that the image of the mounted warrior predominated. The groupings were a constant reminder of the rigid, hierarchical nature of feudal society: Richard's court, for example, was arranged in a straight line on either side of him. Each lord stood with

101

12. *Richard II* (1981): On the wide Cartoucherie stage Bolingbroke (Cyrille Bosc), extreme left, and Richard (Georges Bigot), centre, express emotional states through physical gesture

knees splayed and palms on thighs, remaining within the limits of the lists or paths laid out by black strips running the length of the stage from back to front in the otherwise uniform brown matting. The back wall, behind the stage, was covered with enormous coloured drapes of the finest silk, which fluttered down to suggest a change of location at the end of each scene. The strong use of sound, colour, space and rich fabrics exerted a considerable sensuous appeal and offered visual images that did not pale into insignificance beside the richness of Shakespeare's verbal imagery. One theatre critic evoked the experience as follows:

Into this sublime arena comes rushing a dream-like

cavalcade of Elizabethan samurai; they freeze for a
moment in front of the audience, still wild though
motionless like strangely sumptuous bronze beasts, their
faces painted like masks, their ruffs an added reminder
of characters from Rembrandt. . . . And what a stream
of lyrical images! – Visions which are among the most
dazzling that I have experienced in the theatre: the
challenges in the lists, the stylised cavalcades, the two

13. *Richard II*: Georges Bigot leading a stylised
     cavalcade

tortured favourites of the king turning in a great wheel
and Richard restrained by immense ropes, and the
adventurer who has won the throne kissing the naked
body of the young murdered king, draped across his
knees as in a *pietà*.[8]

The same critic had reservations, however: he complained
that the stylised monotonous diction was a mistake, as it

ironed out the differences between the characters: they lost their specific qualities, and hence the issues around which the dramatic action turns, both political and erotic, were blunted.

This is fair criticism, since Mnouchkine's whole approach to the play appeared to be based on a disconcerting nostalgia for the feudal concept of regal power – a concept hardly different from the image of the king as good shepherd that had been undercut so effectively in *1789*. In the decade separating 1981 from 1971, Mnouchkine appears to have swung full circle, from the demystification of paternalistic feudal relations to an admiration, even a nostalgia for them: interviewed in *Le Monde* (24 November 1981) she declared, 'Shakespeare transports me back to a civilisation and a culture from which I have been liberated – or cut off.' She responded to the powerful identification in Shakespeare's text between Richard and the land, drawing a parallel with a Chinese emperor who had to plough the first furrow and spill his seed in it if a prosperous harvest was to follow. This identification of monarch and land was to be an essential element of the Sihanouk play. The Christ-like image of the dead Richard fitted perfectly with Mnouchkine's interpretation, leaving the audience with an immensely moving image of the divine right of kings – a somewhat bizarre conclusion to emerge from the work of an ostensibly left-wing company.

The production of *Twelfth Night* followed, six months later, in July 1982. Originally the plan had been to present this with an all-female cast, thus giving work for the women so conspicuously absent from the cast-list of *Richard II*. In the event, there were only two male roles taken by women: those of Sir Andrew Aguecheek (Clémentine Yelnik) and Curio (Hélène Cinque). In *Richard II* the stage language had been largely borrowed from Japanese convention, albeit in a somewhat eclectic mix. For *Twelfth Night* the costumes and accompanying music made reference to India, but the methods of stage representation could not be said to have been borrowed from Indian theatre. Where the key directorial concept of *Richard II* had been admiration for power, here it was quite different, focusing on the ambiguities of love. The same stage and the same runways were used; colour and fabric were exploited to equally impressive effect. For Viola's entry in the second scene, a brilliant blue billowing silk cloth was used, from which Viola and her captain emerged, as from the waves on the seashore. Because of the play's predominantly comic tone, there were possibilities, here, for a more flexible handling of the stage space, with even some humorous references to the fearsome warriors of *Richard II*. Feste, the clown, instead of careering along the runway, shot up into the air from a concealed position behind it like a jack-in-the-box. Georges Bigot, as Orsino (who had also played Richard), made his initial entry slowly and despondently, dragging an exaggeratedly long handkerchief behind him to the sound of a grotesque wailing motif from Jean-Jacques Lemêtre: here was an idle aristocrat in love with his own love-sickness.

Mnouchkine's considerable gift for directing comedy emerged strongly, as did Shakespeare's central theme – that love is an irrational force, blinding us to realities. The performances of Philippe Hottier (Sir Toby Belch), Clémentine Yelnik (Sir Andrew Aguecheek) and other members of Olivia's household were developed through clown improvisations and revealed one of Mnouchkine's regular preoccupations: the concern with theatrical transposition. In this play about love and desire the constant element she discovered was that of disguise and travesty. Viola's disguise was presented as the poetic symbol of her journey into the unpredictable land of love. Any hints of homosexuality were underlined: Antonio's lines on meeting Sebastian in Act III, scene iii – 'I could not stay behind you: my desire, / more sharp than filed steel, did spur me forth' – were declaimed with an intensity of affection which suggested a great deal more than just friendship. Similarly, the scenes in which Olivia makes love to Viola dressed up as Cesario suggested that she almost knew Viola was no man. These effects were reinforced by the intensely physical manner in which they were performed. The production concluded with all the main characters moving backwards, hand in hand, to be engulfed in a billowing pink cloth, a reminder of the blue one from which Viola had first emerged. But none of them looked fulfilled: Sebastian kept gazing towards Antonio, while Viola and Olivia turned, perplexed, towards one another, and Orsino seemed equally uncertain.

Many of the weaknesses of Mnouchkine's approach to *Richard II* now emerged as strengths. She described Illyria as a country situated far away in the depths of our profoundest desires and dreams and this was exactly the impression conveyed by her inventive use of movement, gesture and colour on the great open space of the Cartoucherie stage. The vagueness of the setting had detracted from the political realities of *Richard II*; here it appropriately suggested a fairytale world, both nowhere and everywhere. The diction was less monotonous, the musical accompaniment more flexible, capable both of interpreting the characters' moods and of commenting on them. The dazzling images were not there simply to impress, but were constantly calling attention to something hidden behind their seductive surfaces. In *Twelfth Night*

Mnouchkine was able to re-establish some of the double focus which had made *1789* so impressive.

The last of the Shakespeare cycle to be performed was *Henry IV* (Part 1). This opened in January 1984 and closed at the end of the summer, when Philippe Hottier left the company and plans for the other Shakespeare plays were abandoned. *Henry IV* combined successful elements from both of the previous productions; the battle scenes were particularly effective, since the darting, angular and ritualised movements of the actors conveyed just the right sense of sudden, bloody encounter preceded by verbal challenge and followed by pauses for commentary or reflection. Unfortunately the presentation of character through external gesture again developed a theatre of types: the monotonous tavern scenes and the celebrated scene (Part 1, II, iv) in which first Falstaff then Hal impersonates Henry IV carried none of the subtle psychological and political overtones of Planchon's 1957 production. The scene of the Gadshill robbery, however, was memorable for an extended passage of comic mime, in which Falstaff and his friends were cheated of their booty by Hal and Poins. But, from the point of view of the director's art, *Henry IV* mixed together the same elements as in the two previous productions rather than introducing anything new, which did not prevent it from enjoying a huge success with critics and public alike. During 1984 all three plays were performed in repertory to permanently full houses, and in the summer the company was invited to perform in Los Angeles as part of the cultural sideshows to the Olympic Games. Mnouchkine could well have exploited this success for another year, but she was impatient to return to her project for a contemporary play. Finding that she was still not progressing with her own attempts to write, she commissioned a play from her close friend the writer Hélène Cixous.

During the autumn of 1984 the company set to work on researching the history of Cambodia; this was a different process from the work fifteen years earlier on the French Revolution. The point of this research was not to construct improvisations or compose a performance, but to equip the performers to flesh out Cixous's text. Mnouchkine appreciated the play's absence of ideology, saying, 'Hélène Cixous has had the courage to write a real play, with passion. . . . No, it is not Brechtian. There is no ideology.'[9] She found the process of work on the play emotionally demanding and spoke of how the whole company would frequently break into tears. The sentimentalism which has always threatened to engulf Mnouchkine's work was here more than ever a danger. To some extent she was aware of this, recognising the difficulties of approaching a contemporary subject: not being set at a distance in time, the necessary theatrical transposition was, she said, more difficult to achieve.

The visual aspect of the production was certainly one of its weakest points. The enormous stage used for Shakespeare was retained, but the space was not used in the same way: for most of the play the actors were placed on the front three feet of the stage with a vast empty area behind them. Often they were strung out in a straight line, perhaps an attempt to recall the formal groupings of *Richard II*; but, without the same use of stylised movement, these lines of characters simply became tedious to the eye. Some of the entrances were still made on the run, but, instead of coming along a built-up runway, the actors approached from back to front along the wall beside the stage; instead of making a show of force, these long entrances seemed merely awkward.

In interviews coinciding with the opening of the play, Mnouchkine revealed that she had identified wholeheartedly with Sihanouk and the Cambodian people. The one character she claimed to hate absolutely was Kissinger, and this was evident from the one-dimensional presentation of all the scenes portraying him with the generals of the Pentagon. These were lit from below to give them an infernal appearance, while the characters ranted like devils in a morality play. Mnouchkine's affection for Sihanouk, despite his evident weaknesses, was also clear in certain endearing mannerisms of Georges Bigot (who played the part) – for example, a tendency to do a little child-like jig whenever he approved of the turn of political events.

Mnouchkine's comments about absence of ideology and her nostalgia for Sihanouk's paternalistic paradise, swept away by the struggle between modern capitalism and communism, suggest a cause for the failure of this production in Mnouchkine's yearning for utopia. At the end of the 1960s she had been caught up, like so many others, in the enthusiasm for a new world, where revolution would not end until 'the perfection of happiness' was achieved. Twenty years later she could not avoid the guilty knowledge that such utopian enthusiasms had taken a murderous toll in South East Asia. In this way generous enthusiasm for permanent revolution can find itself transformed into nostalgia for feudalism. Indeed the change extends beyond Mnouchkine's personal attitudes to her relations with the whole community of the Théâtre du Soleil. Her proud boast had always been that the utopian vision could be put into practice here and now inside the company: hence the insistence on equal salaries and on everyone taking a turn at every job. Yet the paradox of this community is that almost the only stable element has been

Mnouchkine herself. Of the others, few have stayed for more than ten years and most have moved on more quickly. Behind the depiction of the relationships between the eccentric but gifted Sihanouk and his unworthy lieutenants hovers the image of Mnouchkine struggling to hold her company together while remaining true to her vision.

Perhaps there is a parallel to be drawn with Stein's production of Genet's *The Blacks*. Just as Stein's company felt it necessary to travel to Africa, to black up, to identify totally with the negro race, so Mnouchkine's company identified with Sihanouk's Cambodia and made themselves up to look like the real thing – black, glossy hair, false, protruding teeth, bronze skin. It became almost impossible for a French audience to leave the theatre with an attitude that was anything other than patronising. The applause for Sihanouk at the end expressed sympathy for his plight: it had nothing to do with pity, terror or understanding but remained at the level of Victorian charitable benevolence, a warm feeling of having identified a deserving victim and come down on the side of the angels. The more sceptical spectator was left to wonder whether it was only by getting into the skin of another race that the company could retain its belief in community. Something of this was expressed by John Peter in his review for the *Sunday Times* (5 January 1986): 'This vast episodic chronicle is essentially for whites only. It is both the product of, and an opiate for, the liberal-minded European's feeling of guilt over a small and distant country of which he knows next to nothing, and which his political and military representatives helped to destroy.'

With the change in political orientation, there has been a change in the whole atmosphere of a performance at the Cartoucherie: what began as an openness to all comers has turned into its own peculiar mystique. For *Norodom*

Sihanouk the actors, though still exposed to the spectators' gaze, made up behind an invisible barrier of oriental mystery, each sitting in a careful cross-legged pose. Philippe Hottier has accused Mnouchkine of deliberately generating a myth: 'Ariane is rarely available to do the things she expects of others. It's not that she gets out of jobs. She takes them on when they contribute to her role, her myth.'[10] Hottier's description of the company suggests a group in which everyone plays a role all the time: everyone plays at being part of a collective where everything is open and all power is shared equally. In fact, he suggests, every decision of any importance is taken by Mnouchkine; sooner or later the strain of maintaining the pretence becomes too great, and that is when actors leave.

Doubtless it is unfair to hold Mnouchkine solely responsible for failing to create the ideal society, especially when there are other members of the company, such as Georges Bigot, whose admiration is unbounded, but she invites these criticisms by laying so much emphasis on the life of the group: 'I cannot imagine working in theatre except with this company . . . a company is a school, a school of theatre, a school of life, in any case a communal life of exchange and sharing.' When her interviewer suggested that what she had created was not so much a theatre company in the usual sense, more a 'sort of permanent theatre school', she agreed: 'That's what it has always been.'[11] Mnouchkine may have started out as a political director; certainly in *The Kitchen* and *1789* she developed new forms of expression for political theatre. But since then her work has acquired a more pedagogic slant. Like Copeau between the wars, her authority and the mystique attached to her name increase with every passing year, but it is at the expense of the creative originality of her work as a director.

5
Jerzy Grotowski

Of all the directors under discussion in the book, none has enraged and engaged the imaginations of theatre practitioners and audiences over the past 20 years as profoundly as Jerzy Grotowski. Starting out as a director quite content to treat his actors as his raw material, he has changed and developed to the point where he now sees his role as simply that of a catalyst of others' creativity. The major performances by his Laboratory Theatre – *Akropolis*, *The Constant Prince*, *Apocalypsis cum Figuris* – served as slaps in the face of the largely unfocused and complacent experimental theatre that mushroomed worldwide in the 1960s. The rigorous exigencies of his ethic have had extensive repercussions for the members of his group, carrying them beyond the domain of theatre, determining a way of life. However, despite the mass of material produced around the 'Grotowski phenomenon', much remains misunderstood or shrouded in the obscurantist mysticism that *appears* to characterise Grotowski's own gnomic utterances (the fruit of a peculiarly Polish blend of Catholicism and existentialism). In this chapter, an attempt will be made to clarify Grotowski's quasi-scientific investigation of the nature of the actor's craft, of the actor–spectator relationship, the evolution of his conception of the director's role in the creative process, and the logic of his subsequent rejection of theatre's inherent limitations in the transition to 'paratheatre' and 'active culture'.[1]

Grotowski was born in August 1933 in Rzeszow, eastern Poland, where he remained throughout the wartime occupation. In 1955, having been awarded an actor's diploma by the State Theatre School of Cracow, he attended a directing course at the State Institution of Theatre Art (GITIS) in Moscow, where he was able to make a thorough study of the work of Stanislavski, Meyerhold and Vakhtangov. During the 'Polish October' period of 1956, he was an active participant in the socialist youth movement, publishing a number of militant articles in support of the process of 'de-Stalinisation'. For the next three years, he continued his director's training at the Stary Teatr in Cracow; his productions included Ionesco's *The Chairs* (1957) and Chekhov's *Uncle Vanya* (1959). (He was eventually to receive his professional director's diploma in 1960). In 1959 he became director of the small provincial Teatr 13 Rzedow (Theatre of 13 Rows) in Opole, Silesia, at the invitation of Ludwik Flaszen, a young critic of some prestige, formerly literary director of Cracow's Slowacki Theatre; Flaszen was to remain Grotowski's literary adviser, confidant and 'devil's advocate' throughout the existence of the theatre laboratory. The Theatre of 13 Rows received a minimal permanent subsidy from the local council, enabling experiment and artistic freedom. With this company in its changing forms over the coming years Grotowski would gradually be able to formulate a new function for theatre, through an obsessively purist re-evaluation of the actor's craft.

In general, the work of this period was an intellectually manipulative and heavily conceptualised theatre of effects and artificiality. It reflected a neo-constructivist emphasis on design and the technical media of production, in which the actor's role was highly structured, disciplined and stylised. Actors were seen as puppets supporting the vision of the director as tyrant and ultimately author of the text of the performance event. The work was also marked by initial experimentation into the possibilities of textual montage, the affective content of spatial relationships, and the allocation of roles to spectators (for example, in Byron's *Cain*, 1960, the spectators were designated as descendants of Cain). These were rather clumsy and fumbling attempts to rediscover a theatre of participation, myth and ritual in which the space itself would be as dynamic a protagonist as any other element. On this level, Grotowski's most accomplished and mature production in this period was of Adam Mickiewicz's *Dziady* (*Forefather's Eve*, 1961). Here at last content began to be indistinguisable from form. Through an exploitation of the play's possibilities for audience participation, the design, by the architect Jerzy Gurawski, integrated the spectators with the action, locating them on chairs in apparently random positions within the performance space. The actors' physical proximity, combined with the obligation to take into account their own observation of other spectators and their reactions, forced the members of the audience into an entirely new relationship of confrontation with Mickiewicz's patriotic 'myth' (*Dziady* is the most performed play from the Romantic period in Poland). This Gustav-Konrad carried a broom on his back, not a cross. In Grotowski's dialectic of 'apotheosis and derision', tragedy was counterpointed with the grotesque, play with holiness.

Early in 1962, shortly before the group changed its name to Laboratory Theatre of 13 Rows, the third season was set under way with a production of *Kordian*, by the Polish Romantic poet Julius Slowacki. Kordian, an idealistic patriot and failed assassin, is committed to an insane asylum for his crimes. Within that environment, his all-consuming passion for self-sacrifice is mocked; he is considered insane and sentenced to death. In Grotowski's version the asylum scenes became the kernel of the drama, the action located entirely within the hospital. In this way, Kordian's manic individualism was presented as the impotent madness of the sick; his spiritual and poetic blood-letting (in the original enacted heroically on Mont Blanc) was here rendered as the prosaic physical pain of his medical treatment on a hospital bed at the hands of tormenting and business-like doctors. Flaszen suggests that Grotowski aimed to analyse 'the meaning of an individual act in an era where collective action and organisation are the guarantees of success. Today, the man who tries to save the world alone is either a child or a madman'.[2] The highly structured staging signalled Grotowski's first successful realisation of his concern to create a new and meaningful spatial relationship for each performance. The floor space was multi-levelled, the only decor made up of hospital bunk beds: both platforms for the action and seats for the spectators, who had roles as patients imposed upon them.

Akropolis, presented at the end of 1962, further investigated from a fresh perspective Grotowski's preoccupation with the spectator–actor relationship, within the framework of an expressionistic and profoundly pessimistic reworking of Stanislaw Wyspianski's text. This material was employed as an instrument of social psychotheraphy, a purge for collective complexes. Directed by Grotowski in collaboration with the celebrated Polish designer Jozef Szajna (and with Eugenio Barba as Grotowski's assistant), this work was to remain in the company repertoire throughout the sixties. During its evolution through five different versions, it was toured internationally; it met with enormous critical acclaim in the West, as well as vehement charges of disturbingly abstract and aesthetic formalism.

Wyspianski's original is constructed around an old Polish tradition that, on Easter Sunday figures from medieval tapestries kept in the Cracow Royal Palace are resurrected in order to perform biblical and mythological episodes. Grotowski's version was as darkly subjective and brutally guilt-laden as a Francis Bacon image. Grotowski seized on a suggestion that Wyspianski had made that the Palace was 'the cemetery of the tribes', a representation of a civilisation's values with which to confront modern experience. He transposed the entire work, using a fragmented montage of the original text, to Auschwitz. Here, timeless myths and impulses could be enacted by representatives of humanity *in extremis* within an infernal environment, the historical turning point that epitomises the crumbling humanist values of the twentieth century. The actors represented the dead; the spectators, seated in isolated groups on raised daïses in and around the central space, were the living, incapable of comprehending the horror embodied by the dead. The spectators were deliberately alienated by the performers, treated as uninitiated outsiders, witnesses from the alien world of everyday life. The two worlds remained mutually exclusive, despite the claustrophobic physical proximity of the performers, heightened by the ceremonial erection of an oppressive architectural structure of ropes and metal pipes around and above the onlookers: the bowels of a crematorium, the Acropolis of our civilisation.

The spectator was impelled to watch with fascinated horror the brutalised actor–prisoner's re-enactment of various myths: the Trojan War, Jacob and the Angel, the Resurrection, here delirious dreams, brief moments of wistful escape from the real world of the camp. These enactments were seen as desperate attempts to find meaning in the poetic figures of myth, to reassert values (for instance, love – Paris and Helen) in a search for salvation. Inevitably homosexual, the love scene was a cruel parody, and the conventional image of the value itself was discredited and degraded. In addition, the enactments were continually ruptured by tortuously stylised and rhythmically insistent scenes of forced labour – echoes of the grotesque irony of the Nazi slogan *Arbeit macht frei* ('Work frees') – which had been developed in exhaustive detail during an improvisational period of rehearsal. The dream-like dissolve from reality in the camp to imaginary mythical reality was frequently highlighted or counterpointed by the actors' repetitive incantation of two focal phrases: 'Our Akropolis' and 'cemetery of the tribes'. Using minimal scenic means – a pile of scrap metal (pipes, a bath tub, a wheelbarrow: all instruments of work or torture), Szajna's stark and anonymous costumes (made of sacking, with wooden clogs as footwear), deeply shadowed expressionist lighting reminiscent of a Goya nightmare – and above all the actors' disciplined corporeal means, the production epitomised Grotowski's central concept of a 'poor theatre'. According to this concept, all that is deemed superfluous to the actors' presence and their manipulation of a limited number of objects (mobile metaphors) has been eliminated. So, for example, the actors employed a stove pipe and a rag to represent the bride Rachel in her

14. *Akropolis* (1962): Cortege of the bride Rachel, represented by a stovepipe. Note the use of facial 'masks'

cortège; such use of compensatory objects was cruelly ironic.

The actors' own expressive possibilities here comprised the development of fixed archetypal 'masks' (death masks) using facial muscles and no make-up; a physical score of precisely choreographed, sculpturally defined movements; and a complex contrapuntal vocal score, composed of inarticulate shrieks, ragged whispers and patterned chants, underpinned by a percussive score of abrasive metallic clankings – words were treated as pre-rational incantation and physical sound. The result was an intricately constructed vision of the darkness of the human condition, an image of humanity destroyed. Contrary to the original, Grotowski's version offered no respite, climaxing in pessimism and death. The Christ–Apollo figure that the

118

exulting prisoners bear aloft to lead them into their future was the limp and headless dummy of a corpse. Their suffering had blinded them to reality. Singing together in jubilation and ecstasy, they processed around the space, disappearing one by one into a large box – the crematorium. The lid banged shut with awesome finality. Seconds later, a gentle voice emerged from the roaring silence to tell us, 'They are gone and the smoke rises in spirals.' As victims of collective myth, their release had proved empty; the pursuit of an illusory ideal had led to the sterility and anonymity of ashes. There could be no applause.

A similar predicament awaits the central eponymous character of *Doctor Faustus*, the group's next production (1963). Grotowski entirely restructured Marlowe's text, placing Faustus's final hours as the opening scene. The tiny number of spectators, sometimes no more than twenty, were invited guests at a last supper, witnesses to Faustus's confessional and darkly magic re-enactment of episodes from his life: a secular passion. They were seated along two central monastic refectory tables (stages for past events, the stations of the cross in Faustus's journey) in unnerving proximity to the action. Faustus himself (Zbigniew Cynkutis) presided at their head on a third, adjoining table: the present. His symbolic costume, reminiscent of the medieval theatre, was the white robe of a Dominican monk, contrasting sharply with the Jesuitical black of the Mephistos (played by both a man and a woman). Further claustrophobic concentration and focus was established in part by the complete absence of scenic properties – the actors created them using only their bodies – and particularly by the compression of the space as a whole within a severe wooden wall-like structure. Much of the vocal score was delivered from behind this screen, surrounding the spectators in a vibrant web of sounds complementing or undercutting the physical images before their eyes; they were placed in the very eye of the storm. Grotowski's overtly manipulative spatial design was intended specifically to provoke and dismay the spectators into authentic human reactions, the actors' aggressive physicality and raw emotionality taking place literally inches from their faces. Within their roles, the actors had prepared beforehand a number of different behavioural possibilities to respond to the limited number of reactions they believed the spectators capable of making.

Typically, Grotowski inverted the myth of Faustus, to confront traditional religious taboos. He presented him as the paradigmatic secular saint, a rebel necromancer and Promethean martyr so obsessed with his search for knowledge and truth that he condemns himself to damnation. However, the individual's self-sacrifice proves to be an act void of meaning in this context. Like Kordian's, Faustus's moment of triumphant resolve and fanatical clarity is illusory, symptomatic of madness. He is both executioner and victim. As he is dragged from the space like an inanimate object, his body an inverted cruciform, 'out of his mouth comes a piercing scream and inhuman, inarticulate noises. Faustus is no longer a man, but a sweating, suffering animal, caught in a trap, a wreck who screams without dignity'.[3]

After a brief and unsuccessful experiment in the possibilities of collective creation entitled *The Hamlet Study* (1964), the group moved their base to Wroclaw, an academic centre in south-west Poland early in 1965. This was followed by a change of name to 'Laboratory Theatre: Institute of Research into Acting Method', a title clearly reflecting the nature of the group's concerns.

Since *Siakuntala* in 1960, Grotowski had been

elaborating systematic actor training for the group. Gradually it had become much more than preparation for performance, rather a *process* comprising an integral part of their daily and individual research work. This training was to bear fruit in the collective public works from 1962 onwards. Grotowski has publicly avowed his debt to the challenge proposed by Stanislavski, in terms of the profundity and rigour of his exploration of the actor's craft and of his incessant reappraisal of what had already been achieved. Yet Grotowski has studiously avoided what he sees as the desecration and assassination of Stanislavski's work in its ossification after his death into a 'method'. He refutes the belief that an ideal system can be built, instead demanding the development of *individual* techniques and methods for confronting and eliminating whatever blocks a person's creative process; everyone's obstacles are different and changing, and individual methods must evolve organically with them. Any universal prescription can only impede authentic self-research (work on oneself) and spontaneous self-expression.

Specific techniques and exercises were nevertheless borrowed, in an adapted form, from a variety of sources. These included the Kathakali dance drama of India, source of the facial masks and the desynchronisation of limbs and face, as independent means of expression, in *Akropolis*. There the actors had presented physical configurations comprising elements of deliberately contrasting emotional content or rhythm – the feet tapping out an expression of joy, the hands a fluttering of insanity, the face locked in anguish. In this way the actors become charged polyphonic images combining contradictory associations. Grotowski also drew upon elements of classical Chinese and Japanese theatre training, hatha yoga, Meyerhold's 'biomechanics', Dullin's rhythm exercises and Delsarte's analysis of 'extrovert' and 'introvert' reactions, as well as the work of certain scientists, psychologists and anthropologists who had studied the nature of human reaction and its relationship to collective myth (for instance, Pavlov and Jung).

The training exercises developed by Grotowski can be divided into two broad categories. First, the *exercises plastiques* comprise a series of fixed forms and kinds of movement, largely independent and arhythmic joint-rotation. As in T'ai Chi, once the forms are mastered they can be employed as springboards to improvisatory exploration of the rhythm of flow, of the composition or order of the forms. Liberation comes from a transcendence of discipline and technique. Such a process entails the rediscovery, each time afresh, of the personal impulses that led to the forms and gave them meaning during the initial period of mastery. Secondly, the *exercises corporels* are a continuous series of acrobatic jumps, somersaults and stands, all aimed at a liberation in relation to space and gravity. They were developed as a means of self-challenge, a provocation to find the courage not to hesitate before the physically (and therefore emotionally) dangerous and unknown. In order to be able to undertake a difficult somersault, the actor has to drop his normal defences and place trust in his body's inherent, animal-like awareness, an intuitive 'intelligence' that would thus be involuntarily activated. Once the somersault has been successfully completed, the actor can become aware of the potential mobility of his self-imposed conception of the boundaries of danger: in addition, a further challenge must be found for him. Grotowski believes that self-fulfilment exists as a possibility only for those ready to probe and extend their own limitations; the process is never-ending. Finally, Grotowski investigated vocal expression through a similar process. By bringing his actors to a recognition and subsequent unblocking of psycho-physiological resistances, he aimed to help them rediscover a 'natural voice' and means of respiration, an authentic *vox humana*, necessarily rooted in the body like all emotional expression.

The sum of this training process served as a continuously reassessed and evolving *approach* to creativity. Its primary aim was not athletic development or even corporeal fluidity, but the search for 'objective' laws and conditions determining or stimulating individual expression – the tuning of an instrument before recital. More particularly it aimed to facilitate the activation of what Grotowski refers to as 'body memory': a natural reservoir of impulses to action and expression stored within the physiological make-up of an individual, an intuitive corporeal 'intelligence'. Grotowski is at pains to underline that memory, in this context, cannot be a function of conscious ideation or intellectual analysis. Body memory is the root of all true expression, for it is the body's own retention of an individual's life experiences encoded into his very cells in a deep associational grammar of rhythms, energies and impulses. It is based on the notion that all emotions are linked with certain kinds of muscular activity or physical configurations. If tapped and expressed externally, pure and communicable signs of an archetypal nature may be released. The points of contact with the practice of a number of different schools of contemporary psychotheraphy are not simply fortuitous, for the actor, guided by Grotowski as teacher–analyst, experiences a long and therapeutic process of psycho-physical release and reintegration, a means of full self-repossession. Grotowski's role in this process is necessarily very different from that of any conventional theatre director. The necessity of fostering a special and intimate relationship with his actors, based on a deep trust with regard to his sensitivity to their individual needs, marked a significant evolution in the group's work by the mid sixties: Grotowski's abdication of a directorial Olympus, supported by the ultimate recognition of the *actor* as supreme creator and of the actor's *presence* as the keystone determining the specificity of theatre. Grotowski has specified the implications of this relationship for him: 'This is not instruction of the pupil but utter opening to another person, in which the phenomenon of "shared or double birth" becomes possible. The actor is reborn – not only as an actor but as a man – and with him I am reborn.'[4]

It is essential to clarify one further and crucial aspect of Grotowski's conception of the training process. Traditionally, actor training in the West is inductive – the acquisition of a series of learnt skills, a 'bag of tricks'. Yet in all Laboratory Theatre training work Grotowski insisted upon a deductive approach – a practical and moral ethic of the *via negativa* (way of negation), characteristic of oriental theatre practitioners and martial artists. Such an approach necessitates the stripping-away of 'how to do', a mask of technique behind which the actor conceals himself, in search of the sincerity, truth and life of an exposed core of psycho-physical impulses. As in alchemy, it is a search for the pure essence, the *substantia prima*, of man. The actor must confront *his own* lies and inhibitions and clear the way for self-transcendence in creativity.

> We must find what it is that hinders him in the way of respiration, movement and – most important of all – human contact. What resistances are there? How can they be eliminated? I want to take away, steal from the

actor all that disturbs him. That which is creative will remain with him. It is a liberation.[5]

Grotowski's descriptions of the process are couched in religious terminology, for he had come to believe that art was by necessity a sacred spiritual undertaking. At the moment of authenticity and transparency that he refers to as the 'total act' (a moment of 'holiness' and 'translumination' in which 'the body vanishes, burns and the spectator sees only a series of visible impulses'), the actor–priest exists as the locus of epiphany. Internal impulse and external expression are synonymous and simultaneous, like a cat jumping or a Kendo swordsman anticipating and parrying his opponent's blow. 'The result is freedom from the time-lapse between inner impulse and outer reaction in such a way that the impulse is already an outer reaction'.[6]

As the Polish critic Jan Blonski has pointed out, implicit within the application of a *via negativa* are the assumptions that latent creative impulses lie dormant within the actor (indeed, are inherent in everyone), and that what remains after the process is common to humanity. The total act – an act of provocation and a public unmasking, a mortification of the flesh enabling spiritual illumination – offers the spectator and actor the possibility of experiencing revelation in exposure and a profound sense of community in shared confrontation. The actor as shaman gives of his own profound self in order to locate the way towards change for the spectator, travelling further on that road in his place. The Theatre Laboratory's next production suggested that the heart of this way lies in what Grotowski sees as the sacrosanctity of self-sacrifice and self-immolation. The act of theatre itself can be a means of salvation for the actor–martyr, a focal point in the creation of a 'secular sacrum' located on a human rather than eschatological level.

The Constant Prince (1965), based on Julius Slowacki's version of Calderón de la Barca's seventeenth-century Spanish original, has come to be recognised as the vindication of Grotowski's theoretical and ethical proselytising and of his group's private practical training. It was almost a year in preparation. In Grotowski's version, only the skeletal scenario and baroque tone of Calderón's work remained, and almost nothing of Slowacki's poetry; what little survived was used musically for emotive impact. The production was wholly freed from its original historico-cultural context. The action comprised the humiliation, acquiescence and symbolic castration of a prisoner by a band of persecutors, followed by (and set against) the torture and murder of a second prisoner – Don Fernando, the constant prince, a figure of uncompromisingly inflexible humility and inspirational spiritual fortitude. Showing no opposition to his fate, he passively accepts the role of martyr, offering love and kindness in response to the brutal authoritarianism of his relentlessly cruel torturers, who, in turn, are increasingly fascinated by his refusal to compromise and his 'otherness'; after his death at their hands, they bemoan his loss. The prince (Ryszard Cieslak) wore only a white loin cloth, a symbol of naked innocence and purity in contrast to the heavy cloaks, knee-length boots and breeches of his tormentors, metonyms of an inquisitorial power. His simplicity immediately sets him apart as an anointed figure in possession of true power; the excess of his treatment magnifies his defenceless nakedness. Unable to influence his spirit, they abuse him physically, in this way ironically functioning as agents of his ecstatic apotheosis. In short, it is the Passion of Christ, for

15a. *The Constant Prince* (1965): Ryszard Cieslak and Rena Mirecka; the actor/martyr abused in a grotesque pietà

this non-conformist set against society finds salvation through mortification and sacrifice.

However, here there was a marked change of emphasis in Grotowski's approach to the theme of sacrifice. In Slowacki's Romantic version, typically the prince had represented Poland, its resistance to oppression and its suffering indelibly stamped on the collective psyche; a nation epitomising Catholic martyrdom. Konrad and Kordian are revisited in this essentially Polish martyr myth, according to Flaszen 'a basic leitmotif of all the performances . . . a very vital myth in our society. It is part of the Pole's subconscious equipment.'[7] Yet in his production Grotowski handled the theme in a less nationalistic, more personal way. Above all, the authenticity of the central actor's psycho-physical confession (for such is the fundamental nature of the 'total act') may be seen as an act of ritual redemption for theatre; the myth of the sanctity of martyrdom is reincarnated in the present in the actor's self-transcendence. Our conception of actor and theatre must die in order to be reborn.

The spectators were removed from the bare playing space, looking down on the action from behind the four high walls of a wooden box. This spatial design evoked associations of spectators at a corrida or medieval bear-baiting pit, voyeurs at a secret rite or onlookers at a surgical operation (Flaszen's programme notes made a link with Rembrandt's *Anatomy of Dr Tulp*). From the evidence of his earlier architectural experiments, Grotowski had concluded that direct emotive participation and psychic proximity would result in this case from a spatial distancing of the spectator and his acceptance of the role of witness–observer. In reality, for the spectator this production was an experience of uncomfortable fascination and guilty (if enforced) passivity, peering from afar at the prince's predicament below.

For Cieslak's magical and luminous performance was the very heart of the work's greatness. Here Grotowski's ethic – the holy actor, the total act – became indissociable from the aesthetic; his metaphysic became a compelling theatrical reality, in which an authentic spiritual act was made flesh in the present. Here the spectator was able to see how performance can be a means of personal expiation, the route to an attainment of self-realisation: the 'means' as 'end', the actor as subject and object of a revelation. Using his naked body and his voice, Cieslak succeeded in giving strikingly expressive form to a personal journey of self-transgression, punctuated by three increasingly climactic monologues, through physical pain and suffering (his skin became marked and sore as he bounced stoically under his tormentors' *real* blows and his self-flagellation) to psychic illumination as a visible totality of body and spirit, conscious and unconscious. Despite the homo-erotic overtones, no trace of narcissism coloured his work. He appeared as if in a trance-like state of grace, possessing numinousness beyong acting and technical perfection. This liberation of raw psychic energy, a sacrifice of the ego by the ego after a lengthy process of dedicated commitment, made his performance flower as a dense spatial poetry of personal associations and suggestive nuances: the perfect externalisation of an inner journey.

How was the actor's role elaborated and articulated during the rehearsal period? Over a period of six months working in private with Grotowski, Cieslak had built up a personal score focusing a network of primary, elemental impulses unleashed in improvisation and concretised in physical action (including attendant and involuntary physiological reactions: for instance, respiratory changes,

15b. *The Constant Prince*: Ryszard Cieslak, the 'holy' actor

profuse sweating, muscular spasms). Grotowski would suggest an image or a fragment of text, related to the tentative scenario he had prepared, a continually reworked montage of the original's essential impulses, for the actor to work and explore. During the actor's work, Grotowski would sit in silence, rarely intervening, to observe and note actions and impulses. Occasionally he would offer a broadly associative image to stimulate Cieslak's own associational response, refloating the exploration when it floundered. The director's role in this process was very different from the manipulative directorial authorship which had been imposed in earlier work, where Grotowski had fixed the actor's roles in a search for a realisation of the effects and images he had predetermined. Here the director was catalyst (provoking the actor's descent into his profound subconscious self), agent of selection and validation of the authenticity and communicability of impulses released in this extreme form of corporeal psychoanalysis; in addition he had to be able to withdraw when necessary so as not to block the flow of the actor's creativity. Grotowski's emphasis throughout was anti-intellectual and experiential: 'I do not believe in the possibility of achieving effects by means of cold calculation'.[8]

Once found in action, a process Grotowski believes only possible in relation to another being – in this case Grotowski himself – the actor's personal motivation would never be vocalised or analysed. Grotowski would locate crucial associational details of a moment of authenticity – an attitude, a rhythm – pointing them out to the actor as possible means of re-entry into the original 'true' impulse. It was then the actor's duty to relocate and reconstitute the detailed psychological processes that had unearthed these crystalline moments in improvisation. Grotowski refers to these moments as 'signs', which are *never* figurative or gestural illustrations of a situation or state to be read literally; rather they are associational motifs in the corporeal–spatial totality of the actor's role, points of contact helping the actor locate his own associational context in the process as a whole, each one an image within its own sphere of transpersonal resonances. The sum of these signs, interwoven from moment to moment by a web of personal associations, is the score (role) of each individual actor, while the sum of individual scores (whose coherence it is the director's task to ensure) constitutes the performance made available to the spectators–witnesses. The lengthy process of repetition and refinement eventually allows the actor's 'score', the artificial disciplining structure, to become fixed, a series of conditioned reflexes thoroughly assimilated and recorded within the body. Actor and role interpenetrate in a structure largely contrived by the actor with the director's guidance and encouragement. In performance, each sign (the 'notes' of the score) must be reinvested with the charge of spontaneity by the actor, retracing his personal route during the original creative process yet fully present in the moment.

Apocalypsis cum Figuris, officially premiered in February 1969, was the final Laboratory Theatre production, a work ultimately taking the area of common concern beyond the confines of theatre.[9] In retrospect, it may be seen as an attempt to pursue the creative process outlined above in an amplified form, to include all of the actors involved in a search through collective creation for a sum of individual 'total acts'. The director's role was neither of instruction nor manipulation, but of respectful expectation and focusing; Grotowski tacitly guided the process, helping the actors to structure their own creative responses. Consistent with the group's obsessive evaluatory dissection of Judaeo-Christian mythology, they took as the starting point for exploration the Gospels – the provisional title during rehearsal – and, above all, the Second Coming. Their aim was to rediscover a contemporary significance in the myths, locating the way in which they lived on in contemporary experience, especially the group's own. Flaszen has explained the group's overriding need to avoid a natural tendency in their work to lapse into 'illustrations of the myth'. Consequently, they had to

> depart from the myth to discover a point of reality – this being the awareness of the consequences of the myth. What would have happened to Christ if he revealed himself nowadays? In a literal way. What would we do with him? How would we see him? Where would he reveal himself? Would he be noticed at all? . . . then it turned out there is a passage in the Gospel: 'I have come and you haven't recognised me.'[10]

Once a physical score had been elaborated and articulated by Grotowski and the actors, the group recognised the need to support certain sections textually. The actors turned to their own concerns, responding to Grotowski's suggestions for areas of search. As a result, the final production contained passages from the Bible, Dostoevsky's *The Brothers Karamazov*, T. S. Eliot's poetry and the writings of the twentieth century ascetic martyr and secular saint Simone Weill: all central voices in the literature of modern human experience, responses to man's evolving relationship with the sacred. Tied to the expressivity of the actors' detailed spatial configurations in performance, the result was a delicately woven web of minutely nuanced mythical and historical motifs and images, a visible equivalent of music or modern poetry in the density and mobility of its associational resonances.

Before the hour-long performance, actors and spectators entered the confined darkness of the playing area together; the spectators, numbering just over a hundred, sat either on benches against the wall or on the floor itself. The only hint of theatrical artifice was in two naked spotlights positioned against, and pointing up, one of the walls. No specific costumes were employed and only minimal props: candles, bread, water, a knife – all elemental and archetypal symbols. Bread, for instance, signified the host, the staff of life; candles, spiritual illumination and enlightenment. Almost all scenic effects were achieved by the actors themselves in exploiting their relationship to the space, the light and, above all, to each other. The action of the performance began unannounced with the emergence from the spectators of a small straggling group of contemporary people, suffering somewhat from the after-effects of drink: Dionysian revellers at the prehistorical source of theatre or merely incarnations of contemporary aimlessness and spiritual emptiness? They came across the solitary figure of a simple tramp ('Ciemny', the Simpleton, played by Cieslak), an innocent and gullible outcast reminiscent of Dostoevsky's 'Idiot'; later he would give voice to the spiritual impotence of Eliot's Gerontion. With bitter and sadistic humour, and a growing suggestion of a deep sense of loss, the group played out fragments of myths at the outsider's expense. For their own entertainment, they enforced the role of the Saviour upon him, subsequently assuming similarly ill-fitting roles of their own (named as Simon Peter, Mary Magdalene, John, Judas and Lazarus). Manifesting an overpowering need to be accepted by others, the Simpleton willingly submitted to the role conferred upon him, increasingly suffering physical and intellectual abuse from the others as the role gradually entrapped him. However, the other roles also had an innate life of their own, struggling to possess the individuals involved; the game became ever more serious and dangerous.

The main body of the performance presented the characters' blasphemous struggles to accept or fight against the attractive but enmeshing allure of these roles. For example, Simon Peter was a cynical intellectual, cipher of the existential anguish felt by Dostoevsky's Grand Inquisitor under the burden of freedom of choice; Mary Magdalene was a sleezily sensual procuress, insistent upon a literal and profane embodiment of Christian spiritual love in an act of enforced physical sex with the Simpleton,

16. *Apocalypsis cum Figuris* (1969): Ryszard Cieslak (the simpleton) and Elizabeth Albahaca (Mary Magdalene); the theatre event as meeting place

further debased by the gloating and snickering of the others looking on; she found her voice in the Song of Solomon. Eventually they were all consumed, and in growing darkness the action closely followed Gospel accounts of Jesus's final hours from the Last Supper to the Crucifixion, in the equivalent of which the Simpleton was garrotted. Simon Peter's final words filled the darkness: 'Go, and come no more.' The lights immediately came full up, the space was empty but for the debris of desecration: spilt wax and water, sodden and violated pieces of bread. The spectators were left stunned and alone to assimilate what they had witnessed. For some, it was an exploration of certain underlying psychological needs, elements of psychoanalytic transference taking form as a contemporary passion play, a bitter dirge for a paradise lost. Seen in this way, the play's blasphemous quality was symptomatic of confessional nostalgia, a means of reinstating values, in this celebration of the primordial instinct to lend meaning to experience by linking it to mythopoeic impulses within. For others, the play was a tragic farce, a collective exorcism of the imprisoning and illusory attraction of communing with ancient myths and motivation. The ambiguity was deliberate and necessary. For all, it was a validation of the possibility of direct human communication in a literal tangible event; something authentic had happened. The affective charge of the actors' presence, their emotive proximity freed from the insulation of so many of the trappings of conventional theatre and culture, left few unmoved.

In its evolving form over the next twelve years of its existence in performance, *Apocalypsis* came to represent for Grotowski a potential meeting place, a point of conjunction offering a further blurring, and ultimate elimination, of barriers separating actor from passive observer. The very nature of this evolution, besides investing the actors' relationship to their roles with new life, reflected the changing priorities within the group. It comprised the elimination of all traces of artificial theatricality and of the construction of an 'artistic' object to be appraised: for instance, originally the actors had worn symbolic costumes (all dressed in white apart from the 'outsider' Simpleton, in black with a white stick) and the spectators had sat on benches, which tended to inhibit participation. By the mid seventies, participation was tacitly encouraged at performances. By that time, *Apocalypsis* was only performed as a prelude to inviting all those interested in participation to undertake further work with the group. The play's final performance came in 1979.

During the late sixties, Grotowski had become increasingly frustrated and disillusioned by the divisive limitations of theatre practice. He was saddened by the result of his group's extensive world tours and the dissemination of his own writings. The superficial trappings of the original work had been consumed, and had remained undigested, by 'disciples', particularly in America. They had ignored his insistence on the ethical foundations and responsible inner commitment underpinning these forms, without which they would collapse into ersatz expressionism and 'ecstatic' clichés denuded of any true impulse to ecstasy. Such work was a 'dance of whores'.

A second factor determining Grotowski's movement away from theatre stemmed from his vision of theatre as an arena for researching the quality of contact between actor and spectator. By 1965, his aesthetic had evolved as far as the realisation of a 'total act' by the actor, which he believed offered a provocation to a particular kind of spectator: one willing to 'disarm' by confronting his own motivations beneath the social mask, one who has genuine spiritual needs and who really wishes, through confrontation with the performance, to analyse himself . . . , who undergoes an endless process of self-development, whose unrest is not general but directed towards a search for the truth about himself and his mission in life[11]

Grotowski believed that the total act would be an inspirational gesture of 'positive disintegration', a painful public confession of physio-psychotherapeutic value to the actor. As witness to the act, the spectator would be denied the security of an artificially imposed role – he was simply a human being present in the same space and time. Potentially he could meet the challenge of the act, in turn undertaking a similar process in an attempt to locate and transcend his own personal limitations. Such was the theory. In practice, Grotowski discovered that the very authenticity of the act reinforced and accentuated theatre's basic division into active and passive. The challenge would often lock the spectator into a kind of admiring but resentful distantiation, preventing the encounter that Grotowski repeatedly underlines as the core of any act of theatre. His logical conclusion was the need to redefine the structure of the work (theatre), and to develop instead a new form and a new relationship capable of assimilating those present who wanted to leave their traditional passivity behind.

Most importantly, Grotowski recognised the *process* of fostering and developing a special relationship between actor and director as human beings to be the most valuable element in his work. When this process was part of the production of a performance – an art product – traces of manipulation in the shaping of the artefact necessarily remained. The actor's impulses were somewhat re-formed in the structuring of a sequence of signs and ultimately of his role. As a *human being*, Grotowski felt unwilling to impinge in that way for the sake of a piece of theatre. He felt that his intrusion falsified and despoiled the creative relationship of human being communicating with human being.

> I am interested in the actor because he is a human being. This involves . . . my meeting with another person, the contact, the mutual feeling of comprehension and the impression created by the fact that we open ourselves to another being, that we try to understand him: in short, the surmounting of our solitude.[12]

If art is 'a play between manipulation and inspiration', then Grotowski had to forsake manipulation – and therefore art – in favour of the search for a way of life permitting the reality of inspiration: the eradication of product in favour of process. There could be no more theatre. In 1970, after a solitary journey in India and Kurdistan, he announced in a statement made at New York University and subsequently published as 'Holiday', his abandonment of theatre as the means of his search. It had become a 'ghost-town' for him: 'I am not interested in the theatre anymore, only in what I can do leaving theatre behind'.[13] At the same time, he asserted that the fundamental aim of the search remained the same: what were the conditions permitting human beings to meet and reveal to one another their authentic personal motivations – 'man as he is in his totality'[14] – without fear?

Grotwoski's pronouncements at this time were associative and paradoxical. Those who were able to find an intuitive echo for their own aspirations and needs in his

words, those who felt in some way akin, would eventually
be invited to participate directly in a search for

> games, frolics, life, our kind, ducking, flight; man-bird,
> man-colt, man-wind, man-sun, man-brother. And here
> is the most essential, central: brother. This contains 'the
> likeness of God', giving and man; but also the brother of
> earth, the brother of senses, the brother of sun, the
> brother of touch, the brother of Milky Way, the brother
> of grass, the brother of river. Man as he is, whole, so that
> he would not hide himself; and who *lives* and that means
> – *not everyone*. Body and blood this is brother, it is the
> bare foot and the naked skin, in which there is brother.
> This, too, is a holiday, to be in the holiday. All this is
> inseparable from meeting. . . . In this meeting, man does
> not refuse himself and does not impose himself. He lets
> himself be touched and does not push with his presence.
> He comes forward and is not afraid of somebody's eyes,
> whole. It is as if one spoke with one's self: you are, so I
> am. And also: I am being born so that you are born, so
> that you become: and also: do not be afraid, I am going
> with you.[15]

The work of the period from 1970 to 1975 has become
known as 'paratheatre'. For the first three years, the group
(now enlarged to fourteen, to include a new generation of
non-actor Laboratory Theatre members) worked in
private. This work was focused around the renovation of a
number of old farm buildings in a rural environment near
Wroclaw; this activity was used as a means of establishing a
different rhythm, and a new relationship between the
group and the natural world and between individual
members. In 1973, the work was opened up to the public in
the first 'special project'. Participation was through a

mutually agreed selection process in which the group looked for individuals not necessarily involved in theatre, but with an appropriately open predisposition, for whom the work would be *necessary*. All of the 'special projects' around the world over the next two years attempted to create conditions mirroring those of the group's own rural retreat in Poland; what happened within these conditions remained unprepared. In an isolated but secure environment, they looked for the means of facilitating practical, tangible experience, tacitly encouraging participants to channel any innate impulses into dynamic physical action: work or play. (In this respect, the group's aims were similar to the self-actualisation at the heart of much humanistic psychology, encounter and release therapy.) Space and action were literal, not symbolic, as in most theatre. Simple activities, conducted almost entirely without words, included digging, chopping wood, communal eating and washing. The normal frames of reference of alienated urban man were deliberately dislocated, and all supports and socially acceptable cushions to experience were removed; neither watches nor stimulants were permitted. The group was attempting to create a natural human rhythm, freed from normal social constraints and determined by the body's own impulses: an animal rhythm of waking, working, resting and sleeping.

In June 1975, this initial period of paratheatre reached its climax with the University of Research of the Theatre of Nations, held at Wroclaw. The fruit of private and small-scale work was made available to a wider group, numbering over 5000. There were performances, public meetings and private workshops with a number of distinguished directors: Eugenio Barba, Jean-Louis Barrault, Peter Brook, Joseph Chaikin, André Gregory, Luca Ronconi. Specialists from psychology, anthropology and medicine were also invited. Every day, consultative workshops and seminars with Grotowski and other members of the Laboratory Theatre took place; every evening, a different group or individual led paratheatrical sessions, called *uls* (beehives). There were also a number of smaller, more private paratheatrical exercises in neighbouring rural areas.

The next period of work, until 1977, was focused around *Mountain Project*, directed by Jacek Zmyslowski, a Pole in his early twenties; Grotowski kept a close eye on the development of the work. The project was divided into three distinct steps; each step (and, indeed, each project as a whole) was necessarily unique, its content determined to a large degree by its participants. The first section, *Night Vigil*, took place in Wroclaw: a night of free, silent improvisation served to determine the participants' suitability and readiness to proceed to *The Way*, the second stage. This comprised a journey of 'pilgrimage', on foot, across unknown country to a mountain. The route was physically exhausting, the distance sufficient to necessitate spending at least one night in the forest. The final section, *Mountain of Flame*, saw the pilgrims' arrival at their goal, a ruined and partially renovated castle (lent to the Laboratory Theatre by the state) at the summit of a heavily wooded mountain. The castle contained spaces for improvisatory work, stimulated by the participants' sense of release at overcoming the demands made on them to reach their goal, and by the intimacy born from shared extreme experience.

After 1977, the members of the group researched increasingly divergent and specialised areas of work, although retaining a common aim: the search for conditions encouraging the opening of innate energy enabling a meeting and co-creation with another, a genuine inter-human exchange in which exchange itself was the content. Posters from this period describe the Laboratory Theatre as 'an institute involved in a cultural investigation of the peripheral areas of art and in particular of theatre'; Grotowski renamed the work 'active culture'. Its climax came in a project entitled *Tree of People* (1979), a participatory work involving a large number, in which all elements of collective life were located *within* the work process.

Since 1977, Grotowski himself has led a more intimate, closed research project investigating individual processes within a variety of traditional, ritual means of awakening perception and presence. From 1978 to 1982, the 'Theatre of Sources' (*Teatr Zrodeł*) was to occupy him and an intercultural group of specialist practitioners (including Japanese, Haitians, Indians, Balinese and Mexican Indians) both in Poland and abroad. They studied archaic cultures' active 'techniques of sources' (yoga, Haitian voodoo, Sufi whirling, Zazen meditation, martial arts training) with the intention of locating the pure primordial impulses of celebration and meditation. All of these techniques seek to animate spiritual aspirations and a prerational numinous inner life by means of precise physiological movements and actions: movement as perception. Together with his group, Grotowski developed a series of simple movements and activities, in appearance similar to T'ai Chi or yoga. In 1980 an open group tested them for their accessibility, immediacy and meaning for others. Results were inconclusive, and Grotowski's research continues to this day (1987). In 1983 he became professor at the School of Fine Arts at the University of California, Irvine, where he currently leads a long-term research project.

In August 1984, exactly twenty-five years after the inception of work at Opole's Theatre of 13 Rows, the

Laboratory Theatre officially announced its dissolution. As a cohesive unit it has ceased to exist. It is too early to assess the implications of its members' recent and current concerns. The development of its director shows how a concern for truth in performance and in actor–audience relationships can lead away from theatre to a broader concern for authenticity in human relationships at large.

6
Peter Brook

Peter Brook is one of the most versatile of contemporary theatre directors. In an enormously productive career he has directed more than sixty theatre productions, eight operas and eleven films. Since his work in the 1950s and 1960s is well documented, this chapter will provide an outline of his concerns and practice from *A Midsummer Night's Dream* in 1970 to *The Mahabharata* in 1986. Brook was intensely impressed in the 1960s with the work of Grotowski, whom he invited to conduct workshops with the Royal Shakespeare Company actors involved in his *US* project. Like the Polish director, Brook came to see the actor as ultimately the only source of creativity in the theatre. Without going so far as to abandon production, Brook has nevertheless refined his role to the point where he works principally as a catalyst to his actors' creativity. His art is also marked, however, by his own ethical concerns and has increasingly become a vehicle for spiritual search, both for himself and for the members of his international research group.

In all of his work, Brook has looked for a renewed theatre language as penetrating, rich and alive as that of the Elizabethan theatre in general, and of Shakespeare in particular. Taken together, he sees Shakespeare's plays forming a *teatrum mundi*, a global vision of the different aspects of the real world. Such theatre exists both as ideal and as permanent challenge for Brook, because of the density and totality of experience expressed and because it combines the most popular theatre with the most esoteric theatre that we know in any living language. Brook's admiration for Shakespeare is similar to that of Planchon: in Shakespeare's exploration of man's relation to society, and society's to the universe as a whole, the private and intimate balance the public and epic to form a coherent totality. As a result, his work is 'more realistic than any form of writing before or since, because it can give you simultaneously the surface image in a context, and also tremendously dense information about things unseen and unspoken'.[1] The freedom of a non-localised undefined stage space and a constantly shifting viewpoint means that no single authorial voice is imposed upon us, the apparent objectivity or anonymity augmenting the universality. Brook insists that, whenever any single form or style is imposed on Shakespeare's work, it inevitably results in a restricted, reduced version of the original. The director's and actor's task is to attempt throughout to 'capture in [their] net the richest amount of the contradictory, clashing, opposed, discordant elements that criss-cross these plays'.[2] Brook's grail-like quest for totality in theatrical expression, his desire to reflect a fuller texture of life, as he believes Shakespeare had, is seen by him as an attempt to find the possibility of being for a brief, privileged moment 'at the meeting-points between the two worlds that we crudely call the everyday and the not-everyday, the visible and the invisible'. For Brook, all art aims at a sudden opening of everyday perception, a movement through the recognisable everyday world of material actions to something 'holy' beyond, a mysterious world of 'forms beyond form'.

A Midsummer Night's Dream exists today as a work encrusted with cultural accretions (the cloying residue of nineteenth-century Romanticism, as expressed in Mendelssohn's music, or the flavour of such epic production pieces as Max Reinhardt's celebrated 1935 film version). For his 1970 Stratford production Brook determined to find the 'secret play' beneath, discovering and uncovering the play's living kernel. For him, there could be no gauze-winged fairies or cumbersome forestry. Instead, this was to be a 'defoliated *Dream*', its heart exposed in a new fresh way through a process of elimination of the play's accumulated baggage of denaturing impositions. It would have to be made available and alive to all. This process of elimination and refinement to an essence, unencumbered by broadly accepted stylistic and formal cultural criteria, has characterised Brook's approach ever since.

Brook saw the play as a celebration of pure theatricality, an expression of the liberating joy of 'play', an ode to both actor and the performing arts. As a result, the general tone of his production was of wildly anarchic exuberance, uninhibited physical inventiveness and magical simplicity. The production's starting point was in an attempt to discover what a contemporary notion of magic could be; how would it be experienced directly by a modern audience? Included in the Stratford programme were the following words from *The Empty Space*:

Once, the theatre could begin as magic; magic at the

sacred festival, or magic as the footlights came up. Today, it is the other way round. . . . We must open our empty hands and show that there is really nothing up our sleeves. Only then can we begin.[3]

The mechanics of the magic would have to be clearly presented to all; only then could the invisible become visible. So, Oberon's magic flower ('love-in-idleness') was a spinning, humming silver dish passed between the clear plastic 'wands' of Puck and Oberon. By uniting a conventional conjuring trick with the acrobatic finesse of the Chinese circus, Brook was attempting to bring back 'the gasp of joy, of pleasure. It had to be the right thing to delight, and still suggest what it was supposed to be.'[4]

Similarly, the trees of the labyrinthine forest in which the dream-entangled lovers wander, sleep, hide and make their asides could not be represented naturalistically. To Brook, they suggested fear of the unknown, the teeming darkness of the night and of the hidden sides of human consciousness, and the misunderstandings of love. So in performance they were lengths of coiled wire, openly operated by the fairies from a catwalk above the set. Although transparent, they divided up the space, creating the impression of comprehensible 'real' obstructions with an evil, malignant life of their own. Vertical space was further filled by suspending Titania's red ostrich-feather bower above the stage, and by using circus elements, including trapezes, stilts and ropes. All of these unite magic and danger, as well as acting as mediators between natural and supernatural, profane and sacred. The four trapezes ('love seats') were used to reflect in concrete terms the mobility of Shakespeare's thought and to emphasise the dream quality of the performance. Capable of swinging in all directions, they were visibly operated by stagehands, like some massively amplified Bunraku performance. All were suspended from a bridge between two high metal towers attached to either side of the set, a structure once again openly revealed. The effect was of a literal mobile, an innovative visual 'otherness' in itself hypnotic and entrancing. True to the Elizabethan theatre, or the Chinese opera, which had inspired so much of the production's spirit, this was a theatre for the eyes.

An investigation of the dialectic of form and freedom, discipline and spontaneity, is at the very heart of all Brook's work in the theatre. Here the need was for a set which would impose nothing and encourage spontaneity, while at the same time focusing and ordering. Sally Jacobs created just such a synthesis with her brightly lit and non-representational 'box of tricks' – among other things, compared to a gym, a scientific research laboratory, a squash court and an operating theatre. This purely

17.   *A Midsummer Night's Dream* (1970): Design by Sally Jacobs: the Mechanicals rehearse

functional, formally geometrical and acoustically effective white box was a contained empty space. Neutral and non-specific, a void demanding to be filled with movement, it made a thoroughly conducive setting for the 'stage moving picture', essential for communication in the vast Stratford theatre. A metal catwalk on top of the three-sided box reflected the galleried structure of an Elizabethan theatre; it was used throughout by musicians, as it had been in the Elizabethan theatre, and by the fairies. Some actors were virtually omnipresent, totally involved when not 'on-stage', a reflection of the ideal relationship of spectator to stage. Somehow the structure was simultaneously distancing and intimate, as alienating and inviting as a blank page, a fresh canvas or a slate which could be wiped clean constantly.

During the rehearsal period, Brook developed exercises in non-verbal communication, using improvised percussive and vocal music, and circus and *commedia dell'arte* gymnastics as vocabulary. This period also saw the genesis of Brook's use of various stick exercises (reminiscent of the bamboo 'jo' used in a number of martial arts, particularly Aikido) still used by his group today. In conjunction with a number of other 'toys', including the trapezes, spinning plates, balls and hoops, the sticks were used to heighten dexterity and both individual and group awareness through constant practice and familiarisation. They were seen as potential extensions of the physical and emotional self, and objective concretisations of relationships. They were also equated with words, in a practice developed since *Oedipus* in 1968: 'as we passed the sticks from hand to hand, to the rhythm of drums, over long distances and from great heights, so we were to learn to handle words and speeches, experiencing them as a group'.[5]

The emphasis throughout was on the physical and

presentational. It was hoped that Shakespeare's poetry could be liberated from the deadening familiarity of cliché by arriving at a synthesis of bodily and verbal poetry. In rehearsal Brook wrestled to free his actors from the falsifying patterns of conventional Shakespearian diction. On one occasion, while rehearsing the 'wedding scene' of Titania and Bottom, a release of creative energy from within the group led to a sort of revelation, an intuitive insight into the primitive savagery and mischievous joy underpinning the scene. This brief glimpse of how the play could drive actors in a very powerful way was a moment of exhilarating illumination:

> As the group feeling grew, a wild gaiety seized the company. With books in one hand, and a hoop or a cushion in the other, we whipped the play along like some frantic, bobbing top, until it eventually exploded during the Titania/Bottom confrontation in a welter of torn newspaper, cardboard phalluses and Felix Mendelssohn. As the noise and the laughter died away, we looked around the room, and as though awakening from a dream ourselves, we realised that we had been possessed by some wild anarchic force, that we had been in contact with elements of the play that no amount of discussion or carefully plotted production could have revealed.[6]

Like a scientist, Brook tried to set up the right conditions for such 'reactions' to occur within the group. In practice, almost all attempts to recapture the energy and emotions of these initial visions of what could result proved frustrating and painfully difficult. However, in performance this scene remained one of the most explosive and controversial of the production, on account of its visual movement and

18. *A Midsummer Night's Dream*: Bottom is carried off
    to Titania's bower

colour, and its charged and gross sexuality. Used
mockingly, Mendelssohn's Romantic music was
desentimentalised to take on a new life when set beside this
grotesque union. As Bottom (for Brook, a 'copulatory
emblem') was carried off to Titania's bower atop the
fairies' shoulders, one of them thrust his fist between
Bottom's legs from behind to simulate a massive erection,
the knob of which Titania caressed and clasped lustfully.
The confetti and streamers that followed carried with them
a suggestion of sexual release.

In Brook's version of this play of transformations, the
gap between the 'rough' world of the mechanicals and the
'holy' one of the fairies was blurred until they were seen to
be different aspects of the same totality. Indeed, the rare
dignity given to the mechanicals in this production
suggested that simplicity and innocence are more

immediate and truer than the rather twisted sophistications of the court. Throughout the production, the indivisible interrelationship of different aspects of reality was emphasised. Brook was looking for those links that Shakespeare had recognised between the different levels of experience, for what was common to all; the doubling of roles (Theseus–Oberon, Hippolyta–Titania, Philostrate–Puck) established organic ties between them in a concrete way.

At the play's end, this unification was extended to take in the separate worlds of stage and auditorium. As Ronald Bryden suggested in *The Observer* (13 December 1970), 'if you want to demolish the barriers between persons, you're more likely to succeed by the traditional methods of conciliation: offering a show of vulnerability (what else is comedy?), friendliness, play, and finally physical contact'. This production seemed to contain an invitation to join in the fun, the evident joy of performance, just as *Ubu* did in the late seventies. Physical barriers between stage and auditorium were broken down in an entirely non-aggressive manner; for example, Snug's over-enthusiastic lion 'accidentally' fell into the front rows. The final moment was a literal enactment of Puck's 'Give me your hands if we be friends'. The actors jumped down into the auditorium, smiling and shaking hands with all those in reach as they walked past. Here they were reaching towards the communion of a shared, celebratory experience, cemented in the concrete reality of physical contact. In an ecstatic review in *The Times* (30 September 1971), Bernard Levin suggested that the spectators were left at the end with 'a feeling of rebirth into a new, cleansed world of love and joy'.

Since 'Oh! for Empty Seats' (in *Encore*, 1959), Brook had dreamt of being in a position of total subsidy which would free him from the crippling commercial exigencies and impositions particular to the 'glamour circuit'. He was also feeling increasingly strongly that the present set-up of the theatre, with its 'formal institutional apparatus', provided the wrong arena for 'communication, ceremony and involvement'. At the end of 1970, he received unprecedented financial aid (chiefly from the Ford, Gulbenkian and Anderson Foundations, and UNESCO) to assist in the setting up in Paris of the CIRT (Centre International de Recherches Théâtrales), involving a group of actors and directors from as far apart as Japan, Mali, the United States, Britain and France. He was now able to turn his back on the conventional channels and forms within which commercial work – the selling of a product to a consumer market – must remain. Such work could only ever be a corruption or compromise of all that he felt to be valid and alive in theatre. He would now be able to work in a wider variety of conditions, to realise his need to look through theatre for a way to 'evolve something up from the seed; not to add things together, but to make conditions in which something can grow'. Like Grotowski's Laboratory Theatre in Poland, with no obligation to give regular performances and the 'right to fail', the research group would have time to develop and explore material and forms, the effect on the work of differing performance conditions, the nature of the actor's craft and of theatre itself. Now he could be free to investigate a 'deeper chain of rules' separating and uniting human beings the world over, in the pursuit of a truly living theatre of international forms.

The Centre has always had three separate, but equally important, functions to fulfil. First, it has a responsibility to theatre-going audiences, those who keep the theatre in existence. However, Brook's deepest convictions perhaps lie in the other two functions, the first of which is a determination to create a relationship with people who would never normally have any contact with the theatre. Since the LAMDA (London Academy of Music and Dramatic Art) Theatre of Cruelty season (1964), the emphasis of Brook's research had been largely on the preparation of the actor. Around the time of the *Tempest* experiment in 1968, there was a noticeable swing towards an emphasis on the actor in relation to an audience in changing environments and conditions, and on the development of a natural human relationship with each particular audience. This became Brook's central concern in his work throughout the seventies. In the first three years of the Centre's existence its work was structured according to his notion of a 'rhythm in and out of life'; an outward movement into life ('work-in-the-field') was to take the group on a major journey every year (Iran, Africa, America) – exercises in the validation of research work behind closed doors, as well as an infusion of life through exchange. (There are still regular minor sorties to schools, hospitals, prisons, new towns and centres for immigrant workers in the Paris region.) Here the fundamental aim was to explore 'what the conditions were through which theatre could speak directly. In what conditions is it possible for what happens in the theatre experience to originate from a group of actors and be received and shared by spectators without the help and hindrance of shared cultural signs and tokens?'[7]

The third of the Centre's functions lies in the group's responsibility to itself and to its craft. Here the movement is inward, for the actor's research must include self-research and development, a process which can only take place in conducive conditions out of the public eye. Such work – a search for 'processes, combinations, causes and effects hitherto unknown' – is privileged and private, although Brook remains eminently aware of the madness of believing for a moment that theatre work can exist in the absence of a relationship with an audience; isolation turns in on itself. Private research enables elements of theatre to be isolated and placed under a microscope, taken down to their smallest forms to be contained and examined in minute detail to make its true components visible. For Brook, the actor's training, like that of the oriental performer, is not instrumental, a means to an end, but rather a holistic process forming one of the primary means of personal growth: 'a physical approach to understanding', in the words of Yoshi Oida. Like Grotowski, Brook uses exercises and specific techniques (for instance, T'ai Chi Chuan and Dr Moshe Feldenkrais's science of maximum-efficiency body movement) as preparatory approaches to the stimulation of sensitivity, to make of the actor 'a source of natural signs' in the 'total exercise' of performing. The premise of all such work is that the individual is capable of more, of coming closer to a real fulfilment of his potential. Only through extensive and sincere work on himself within a group situation can the individual actor transform his body, the raw material of his craft, into 'an instrument that transmits truth that would otherwise remain out of sight'.

Much of the Centre's research in its early years was taken up with an intense study of minima in expression and communication. A single movement, gesture or sound – even a walk – might be scrutinised for days on end, constantly stripped of parasitic interpretative impulses until the transparent, pure activity remained. Brook has described the aim of all such research work as to make acting less a communication through imitation, and more a form of natural language potentially accessible to all. It was felt that, by isolating certain simple elements of movement or sound, it was possible to arrive at certain full expressions of a state of being with the ability to transcend cultural barriers, to unify in a sudden and mysterious communion. For example, a slowly opening hand perhaps has intercultural associations of growth, opening, come to life; turn the hand around, and there is a story at every moment of its passage through a claw to a fist. No gesture is neutral, without significance; and what happens if you load a gesture with an apparent significance (fist: violence) with an inner dynamic of contrary significance (fist as symptomatic of love or welcome)? Is it communicable?

A form of theatre based largely on language had to be rejected at this stage by the multinational group. As a researcher into non-imitative, intercultural forms of expression, Brook views the value of the word in today's theatre with suspicion and scepticism. Yet, like Artaud, he has never proposed an abolition of language, but believes rather in the need for a critical re-evaluation of its role and fundamental nature. Today the efficiency of the word as communicator appears to be taken for granted. Contact with certain dead languages showed Brook that the world of words had diminished drastically, that, over the passage of time, words have been stripped of taste and substance, leading to 'a gradual reduction of emotional range, emotional capacity, and even emotional–intellectual concentration of meaning *within both actor and word*'.[8] Like *Sire le mot* ('My Lord word'), the actor has in turn become emotionally diluted, unresponsive and one-dimensional. Expressivity has been reduced to a pale, shadowy fragment of its true potential. Nevertheless, as his admiration for Shakespeare's plays shows, Brook recognises that words need not always be the dry and lifeless mechanisms that common usage so often seems determined to make of them. Some words naturally contain a nucleus of sound, a dynamic substratum, whose life is both independent of the word's discursive meaning and at the same time organically linked to it.

Brook's work of the early seventies was built around a series of questions arising from these concerns and convictions. Can certain elements be communicated directly without going through the channels of a single culture's shared linguistic signs? Can the simple relationship of a sound and a movement be charged with a poetic density touching a chord in anybody and everybody, giving rise to one of those moments in which, in Arthur Koestler's words, 'eternity looks through the window of time'? Is there a tonal consciousness common to all? Are there archetypal deep structures of a vocal or gestural kind, dynamic and instinctive? If a true collective expression of the essentially human in experience could be created, Brook's ideal of universal communication would be validated. To achieve this, it would be necessary to elevate above text those elements of communication traditionally considered to be secondary: corporeal gesture, tone, the dynamics of both sound and movement on an individual and a collective level. The actor as a unit would have to ask: what animates man in relation to his culture? what is at the origin of human needs for and manifestations of 'make-believe'? what situations are dramatic on a human level, while remaining areas of true exploration? Inevitably such work must end less often in conclusive answers than in further questions. Brook is more interested in looking for the dynamic processes in the creation of living forms in practical terms, here and now, than in elaborating any kind of system. He believes all visions and realisations to be in themselves necessarily incomplete. All creative artists must remain open to the need for growth, without fanatically defending any one aspect which can only ever be one fragment. For '*the complete truth is global*' and, for Brook, the theatre alone is the place wherein 'the great jigsaw can be played'.[9] His dream remains a 'universal theatre', which he describes as 'theatrical expression more richly in touch with the natural fullness of any human being's potentiality'. His work has consistently thrown down a challenge to 'all the elements that in all countries put the theatre form into a very closed bracket, imprisoning it within a language, within a style, within a social class, within a building, within a certain type of public'.[10]

During its first year, the CIRT created an intensely poetic theatre work for the Shiraz Festival in Iran, a 'high' work made up of mystical and esoteric vocal and gestural abstractions: *Orghast*. With its starting point in the Prometheus myth, this darkly Manichean piece was performed in an invented language of musical phonemes developed by the poet Ted Hughes, in collaboration with the actors in improvisation, and in certain dead languages – Ancient Greek, Latin and Avesta, the extinct hieratic religious language of the Parsee fire prophet Zoroaster. It was an attempt to go back to the very source of language as incantatory sound, when an act of communication had also been an act of communion. 'If you imagine music buried in the earth for a few thousand years, decayed back to its sources, not the perfectly structured thing we know as music, that is what we tried to unearth.'[11] One of Brook's constant ideals has been to locate what in theatrical terms can be conveyed and received as music, that invisible and mysterious language which can surmount barriers imposed by social, linguistic and cultural forms. As a musical form closed to rational analysis, reminiscent of Artaud's jagged glossolalia, many saw *Orghast* as 'a big leap forward for the theatre from representational to abstract, abandoning the meaning of words for their sound. It happened in art 50 years ago, when the form of an object was abandoned for colour and shapes.'[12] However, form and location – the vast open spaces and awesome ruins of Persepolis – condemned *Orghast* to remain hermetically locked in obscurity. Certain potential emotional responses were inevitably precluded; preconditioned dark aesthetic associations and assumptions are attendant upon any treatment of obscure archaic languages, mythology and ritual in a melodramatic tomb setting.

The emphasis in the CIRT's second year, when the group undertook a three-month journey in jeeps across the Sahara and North West Africa, was on simplicity and exuberant naïveté released through *improvisation*. At the genesis of theatre, ritual and ceremony were integral parts in what was a communal religious celebration. The act of theatre was necessary as an organic and spiritual oasis of socially cohesive power, for it possessed a quasi-therapeutic social function. For Brook, however, today in the West 'we do not know how to celebrate because we do not know what to celebrate'. With no agreed matrix of unity, there is only confusion, contradiction and fragmentation. He believes that the theatre today must attempt to redefine the former ceremonial quality particular to it, to continue to try to fulfil its ancient role as a 'religious action', 'that by which fragments are made whole'. He has looked relentlessly for a valid equivalent in today's splintered world of the nature and function of ancient religious theatre: theatre necessary as a source of nourishment and renewal to a community, theatre as the meeting place for a potential restoration of the lost unity of man. Brook suggests that, now that the shared possibility of ritual has been lost to us, the only alternative is through 'a more intense search moment by moment for a quality that is *the sense of the present*, of each moment, in the Zen sense'. In practice, it is in improvisation that he believes he has found an equivalent to ritual, for it has the ability to liberate moments of a dense, communicable and unifying truth in the here and now. Creatively, improvisation is both means and end-in-itself for Brook, the fruit of a one-part theatrical process in which preparation and performance are simultaneous and synonymous. The actual moment of performance is the beginning and end of all: every occasion, setting or audience is different. Improvisation has become the fundamental principle of Brook's experimental practice, which recognises the actor's responsibility as the ultimate source of creativity.

By taking the group to Africa, Brook was consciously putting them in a position of vulnerability where the challenge would be greatest, and therefore the possibility of development richest. In the absence of the complicity that comes from shared cultural references, an equivalent would have to be found in what is essentially human in experience. Yesterday's truth may be meaningless today. Brook was asking his actors to begin again every time from as near as possible to a zero point where nothing could be taken for granted. With only the most skeletal scenario or a simple object (a shoe, a stick, a box, bread) as a starting point for improvisation, they had to find a way to coax that occasion's shared frame of reference into being within the furious passion of performance. In such conditions, highly prepared and polished work was both irrelevant and 'anti-life', while improvised forms were absolutely necessary. The group were obliged to confront their responsibility to create from nothing, entering the empty space – a carpet – and meeting the 'moment of truth'. Naked, defenceless and alone, the actor had to 'seize the current, ride the wind, deal with the forces that are there at that time and only at that time'. He was forced to expose everything to the critical spotlight at the same time: his powers of concentration and imagination, his ability to communicate with clarity, his sense of rhythm in a collective, his openness to life, his courage. Any dogmatic approach would be deadly: 'The training of an actor is like that of a Samurai. It may last for years and years and lead up to one sudden confrontration. The only rule is that one is never prepared for the situation one really meets.'[13]

Africa offered Brook and his actors the opportunity to undertake a quasi-scientific investigation of the nature of improvisation. Above all, he wanted to research the relationship between what has to be prepared and what cannot be prepared, to attempt to find the difficult balance of what is spontaneous, of the moment, and the kind of structuring or ordering which would feed and support that moment without imposing anything, and thereby closing off living impulses. An open non-restrictive form had to be found to encourage the free play of the actor's creative energy, a form at the same time not so loose as to collapse into inarticulate and anarchic diffusion. Like Grotowski, Brook had recognised that, paradoxically, too much freedom is a lack of freedom.

It has become evident that this one journey remains the group's most important collective experience to date. Through shared experience, the actors were able to some degree to regress (in reality, progress, as with Grotowski's Taoist-based process of unlearning, the *via negativa*) to a state of innocence that is a state of natural creativity present in childhood but lost in the passage to adulthood: a direct experiencing of a response to present reality, immersion in present process through the reawakening of an original spontaneity. Africa has had the most profound and visible influence on all of the CIRT's subsequent work.

Certain celebratory and unifying meetings refined the actors' sense of what a relationship with an audience could be, the uncovering and sharing of submerged interrelationships, the joy of participating in a moment of illuminatory creativity. On another and more prosaic level, the nature of the work in Africa has coloured the very texture of the actor's craft in more recent productions. For example, one characteristic of all the work at the Bouffes du Nord (the CIRT's home in Paris) since 1974 is the minimisation of scenic means, the creation of worlds through the manipulation of simple everyday objects: a stripped 'poor' theatre. In the African 'carpet shows', these objects were used as a means of centring, anchoring and focusing collective work as close as possible to a zero point, providing the minimal necessary support. At the same time, they were a source of marvel, a stimulus to the imagination – raw material for full creative exploration.

19a. The shoe show: Improvisation on a carpet in an african village by Helen Mirren, Yoshi Oida

19b. Public demonstration of exercises, April 1972, Récamier theatre, Paris; left to right, Malik Bowens, Bruce Myers, Lou Zeldis

For example, a shoe thrown onto the carpet would create interest demanding development. As the power of focused attention breathed life into the inanimate, the object would undergo a creative transformation. Thus, when an 'old hag' put on the shoe to become young and beautiful, an element of magic accredited to the object by the space was realised in concrete terms. In almost all such improvisations, the object was displaced from its normal functional usage (for instance, the shoe became a musical instrument, drinking vessel, weapon). Through the serious play of make-believe, the evocative resonances within any object can be released; as in children's games, it participates fully. The actors reawaken their capacity for play, their ability to juggle with a simple reality to create something new. The use of objects in this way – as multi-transformable neutral material, both mobile metaphors and metonymic adjuncts referring to a wider social reality – has become an integral part of the group's theatrical practice. *Ubu aux Bouffes* (1977) was to be the clearest and most condensed expression of such work in a full production. Brook succeeded in finding a valid equivalent for Jarry's anarchic linguistic primitivism in the manipulation of found everyday objects (bricks, sticks) dislocated from their normal frame of reference, a new temporary function endlessly redefined for them by the actor.

What of Brook's role in the work of the CIRT? A few influential voices have accused him of being manipulative in his approach, exploiting actors as objects in the enactment of his own obsessive visions. Yet the emphasis placed by Brook on improvisation as the ultimate means of theatrical creation suggests very different qualities in his approach, qualities validated by the actors themselves. He recognises that an actor who brings an openness and conviction to his work can penetrate much deeper towards a position of truth than is ever attainable through directorial imposition. His actors never became what Artaud once cried for, 'neutral pliant factors . . . rigorously denied any individual initiative'.[14] Brook feels that his task consists largely of the creation of situations in which the actor is free and responsible for imaginative investigation, and of the regeneration of this creative process when it founders for whatever reason. Throughout the period of preparation, he attempts to clear the way for expression by offering a series of challenges and shocks to the actor to awaken him to his own possibilities. A sort of catalyst, he provokes, questions and stimulates both body and mind to responses which can never be predetermined. The CIRT's actors see Brook as the least interventionist of directors. He never directs specific moves as responses, instead placing the actor in situations which force him to give of himself totally while retaining a critically lucid awareness concerning the efficacity and clarity of what is expressed.

The nature of the group's recent work has been determined to a large extent by Brook's discovery in 1974 of a derelict nineteenth-century theatre, Les Bouffes du Nord, behind the Gare du Nord in Paris. It had been a theatre of some prestige and history, but fell out of use in 1950 and it was finally abandoned in 1952 due to a fire. It nevertheless closely matched Brook's ideals; to this day it has remained largely as it was after the fire. Although disembowelled and in a state of decay, the spirit of the theatre's past remains. It is above all a place marked by life. Impressions are strangely contradictory, for it appears to be at an indeterminate mid-point between renovation and demolition. It bears the marks of transition from an old to a new world. As such, it provided an ideal space thematically for *Timon of Athens* (1974), *The Iks* (1975), *Ubu aux Bouffes* (1975), *The Conference of the Birds* (1979), *The Cherry Orchard* (1982) and *The Mahabharata* (1985), all of which concern themselves with worlds in transition. No attempt has been made to conceal the remaining evidence of the theatre's past splendour. The towering back wall, over fifty feet high, is scarred and pitted by the wear and tear of the years, like an aged human face. The only sign of the former stage and its machinery is a wide horizontal band traversing the wall and a dark square stain above, framing the old stage picture, like a Turin shroud for a dead form of theatre. The playing area, originally the front stalls and stage, forms an immense empty space; non-specific, neutral and open, it possesses the freedom and infinite transformability of the non-localised Elizabethan theatre.

As if in an enclosed courtyard, performers and public are bathed in the same 'open-air' light throughout. The full horseshoe shape of the ranged benches, situated on the same level as the playing area, and of the three crumbling rococo balconies above gives the theatre the concentration and relationship of direct contact with the spectators that the group had experienced on the carpet within the circle of the African villagers. As a whole, the theatre reflects Brook's desired economy of means, his growing asceticism in the move towards a 'poor' theatre in which the actor is free to communicate directly and intimately. The lesson of Africa was perhaps above all the necessity for reinjecting human content into the theatre at all levels, for placing human beings in relation to each other. Brook describes his work at the Bouffes as an attempt to 'reunite the community, in all its diversity, within the same shared experience'. In all of the Bouffes performances, the spectator is treated with respect, as participant. For the spectator, the result is one of witnessing a magical and unique event of celebration created in and for the specific moment.

One of Brook's first major productions at the Bouffes reflected the anthropological overtones of much of his work since the formation of the CIRT. *The Iks* was an adaptation of Colin Turnbull's best-selling study of the tragic demise of a northern Ugandan tribe, *The Mountain People*. Brook saw this material as a rare meeting point between 'a personal experience, objective facts and poetic, mythic elements' – the concrete reality of an anthropological study, and a parable vision of our own fallen condition and universal predicament, with Turnbull's personal journey into the 'heart of darkness' as the point of union. In performance it became the story of an African tribe told by actors of five different nationalities, for, like all of Brook's work, it is about all of us: 'The Ik survives at a cost – and so do we. The parallels are alarming. The same sort of situation can be seen in western urban life. For me, it's the perfect metaphor: something which exists on two levels – real in the sense of life as we know it, real in the deep sense of myth.'[15] So the performance could be based neither on a cool relating of documentary facts, nor on total impersonation. During an intensive study period, the group copied in great detail the postures and expressions of the Iks as seen in Turnbull's photographs. While the others observed, criticised and corrected, an actor would improvise the action or movement of shortly before and after a photograph. Through this strictly *physiological* and *plastic* approach (and therein lies the change of emphasis from Stanislavski's *emotional* memory), gradually the actor made contact with echoes of his own experience, eventually discovering and, all being well, communicating 'the reality of that hunger, not from an emotion, but from an exact sense inside himself of what it meant to be standing in that position with that part of your body sagging with that part of your mouth open'.[16] A mass of material drawn from episodes in Turnbull's book was thrown up in improvisation; at one point, the actors built and lived in an Ik stockade within the theatre. Although much of this material was later discarded in the refinement process, it had served its purpose of permitting them, to a certain extent, to 'become' Ik. Through this process of 'saturated naturalism', somehow a racially mixed group of actors, using their ordinary clothes and no make-up, transcended their appearances to represent an essence of Ikness recognisable to all.

Brook considered *The Iks* to be in a direct line from *US*, a controversial 'group-happening–collaborative spectacle' devised with the Royal Shakespeare Company in 1966 as an attempt to confront and respond to the Vietnam War. Both drew on immediate and burning socio-political realities, lives still being lived, to create very different forms of what became known in journalistic shorthand as 'theatre of fact'. Both projects were viewed as challenges to find forms of theatrical expression of greater power and directness than conveyed by the surfeit of photo-documentary evidence, to which the West has become insensitive through over-exposure. It is significant that both productions received criticism from the same quarters and for similar reasons. In the case of *The Iks*, Kenneth Tynan attacked Brook's 'shallow and factitious pessimism' and 'amoral misanthropy' in his choice of material and in the depiction of Turnbull's despair. An interpretation of Brook's world-view as one of facile nihilism is indeed understandable in the light of the nature of Brook's thematic material since *King Lear*. He seems to have been fascinated by the belief that, in certain extreme situations, civilising social restraints reveal themselves to be false and shallow, crumbling to unleash the human beast within. From *Lord of the Flies* ('a potted history of man'), his sensory assault version of Weiss's *Marat/Sade* (during which the copulatory revolution of the lunatics continually threatened to spill over into the auditorium) to *The Mahabharata* ('the great poem of the world'), his anti-idealistic bent has chosen to portray, by the death throes of liberal altruism and humanism, the destruction of innocence by experience.

Brook's next work, *Ubu aux Bouffes* (a conflation of Jarry's grotesque Ubu plays), clearly coincided with the vision of the world represented in the cycle of plays at the Bouffes. Ubu is in many ways an Ik; his conception of reality is one-dimensional. His world ignores the possibility of any form of transcendent understanding. Rather it is a world of utter materialism and egotism – the world as stomach. For Brook, the real value of Jarry's work lay in the way in which such themes have been treated. Through a stylisation of Ubu's monstrosity, a disintegration of language and an explosion of traditional forms, the whole was tilted and consequently taken far outside the boundaries of social documentation. The general tone of this 'rough' performance was one of playful invention and music-hall celebration, its frenetic rhythm reminiscent of silent movies. In one scene, for example, Ubu rode on top of an enormous industrial cable spool (his *voiturin à phynances* – royal state chariot, bulldozer and tank), devastating a fragile peasant dwelling. Some of the peasants were crushed as the spool ran over them, emerging in its wake flattened into the ground – an image from Keaton or Tom and Jerry. During a scene of winter snowfall, Ubu tossed a handful of confetti into the air above his head, teeth chattering audibly as it floated down over him. In similar style, the Russian offensive and bombardment of Ubu's army, just two actors in accordance with Jarry's specifications, were conveyed through the dropping of a vast number of silver 'superballs' from the balconies, these 'bombs' bouncing endlessly on the concrete floor and into the audience to Toshi Tsuchitori's percussive accompaniment.

Brook turned next to *The Conference of the Birds*, a twelfth-century Sufi poem by Farid Ud-din 'Attar of Nishapur, a lengthy philosophical and religious fable allegorising the human condition and mankind's search for truth within himself, like Gurdjieff's semi-autobiographical *Meetings with Remarkable Men*, which Brook made into a film in 1977. The elements of struggle and search, the thirst for a beyond, a 'something more', the intercultural bird idiom concretising man's inner

Peter Brook

20. *Ubu aux Bouffes* (1976): Ubu (Andreas Katsulas) on his 'voiturin à Phynances'; below, Yoshi Oida; behind the three balconies of the Bouffes theatre

aspirations, his desire to go beyond himself into 'flight', all, for Brook, offered the possibility of a true theatre of myth and poetry. Constantly returned to as source material for free improvisatory work throughout the seventies (the entire American journey in 1973 was built around performances of the poem in different milieux), *Conference* became for the group a symbol of their work, the focal point for the development of a commitment to their own ideals. At the end of the CIRT's first decade, the poem remained for Brook the only material offering the possibility of approaching his cherished ideal of totality. It was a natural choice for a production which would be a combination, and in some ways a summation, of the different areas of investigation explored so far.

To facilitate the demanding multi-transformation necessitated by the mobile identity of actors as storytellers, for the first time the actors made use of masks and puppets. Brook saw certain ancient Balinese masks as denser, more essential expressions of a human truth: poetry and music, as against the prose of the face. Their intensification of psychological states through simplification took them from the specific to the universal. One scene of great power and simplicity used both mask and puppet forms. The birds, high above the desert in timeless, weightless flight, saw a lone earthbound hermit wandering in the distant void – a figure represented by a tiny Balinese puppet operated by Tapa Sudana. As the birds circled and landed, the puppet was replaced by a masked actor. An appeal was made to the spectator's imaginative participation; he shared the birds' viewpoint, their changing perspective on the tiny solitary figure. An impression of distance covered was made concrete in this naïve and fairy-tale way, both comical and magical.

In 1980, the group took part in the eleventh Adelaide

21. *Conference of the Birds* (1979): The hermit in the desert: Andreas Katsulas is the masked hermit; the birds are: left to right, standing, Alain Maratrat, Miriam Goldschmidt; in front, Malik Bowens, Mireille Maalouf, Bob Lloyd

International Arts Festival in Australia, performing the three major works *Ubu, The Iks* and *Conference*. On the final day, all three were presented as a continuous sequence, a clear statement of the relationship of the parts to the whole. Here was a body of work to be considered together. As a *trilogy*, the plays formed a lucid expression of Brook's social and ethical concerns. Typically, he chose to define all three as live theatre in terms of celebration. The 'pure, rough, crude energy' of *Ubu* expressed the actors' 'celebration of energy'; the heightened naturalism of *The Iks* was a 'celebration of detail'; and, finally, the intercultural significance and accessibility of *Conference* were seen as a 'celebration of the possibility of crossing barriers'.

Since *Conference*, most of the Brook's energy has been devoted to realising for theatre an adaptation of the world's longest narrative poem, the ancient Sanskrit heroic epic *The Mahabharata*. At eighteen volumes and almost 100,000 verses in its full form, it is almost eight times the length of *The Odyssey* and *The Iliad* combined, and four times the length of the Bible. Along with the other Sanskrit epic, *The Ramayana*, it forms the core of Hindu culture in India and throughout South East Asia, where it has become the common source for most of the dramatic material of dance drama (including Kathakali), story-tellers, popular folk players, puppet shows, films and even strip cartoons. It is considered by scholars and public alike as the greatest work of imagination that Asia has produced.

Brook's version was premiered at the 1985 Avignon Festival as a twelve-hour cycle of three plays – *The Game of Dice*, *Exile in the Forest*, *The War* – with a limpid and restrained French text by Brook's collaborator since *Timon of Athens*, Jean-Claude Carrière, formerly Luis Buñel's screenwriter. Three years in the writing and six months in closed rehearsal (with a journey to southern India for everyone involved in the project), the production was immediately hailed as a masterpiece. It was performed in a remote amphitheatrical quarry on the banks of the Rhone south of Avignon, the towering cliff face texturally reminiscent of the scarred and pitted back wall of the Bouffes. Brook believes that, as a vision of a society in disaccord coming to the brink of self-destruction, this 'great poem of the world' (the meaning of the Sanskrit title) offers us the closest mythological reflection of our times. It tells the story of two warring families, the evil Kauravas and their exiled cousins the Pandavas, from their mythical and magical origins to their apocalyptic mutual destruction during an eighteen-day battle on the plains of Kurukshetra. In the tradition of heroic romance, the central narrative is loaded with countless loosely related episodes. Brook and Carrière distilled and refined the material to bare the spine of the central narrative.

In the same way as the work of Shakespeare or Attar, *The Mahabharata* is, in Brook's view 'anonymous', an expression of what is essential in human experience rather than the product of an individual ego; it belongs to the world, not only to India. It is of such scope that it is traditionally proclaimed that 'what is not in *The Mahabharata* is nowhere'. Indeed, Brook suggests that this poem is 'richer in dramatic material than *Conference* and more universal than Shakespeare's complete works'. Private and public, intimate and epic, 'holy' and 'rough' coexist in uncomfortable juxtaposition. The lyricism of poetry (those moments of concentrated focus when one sees more clearly, one breathes more freely) springs from a sharing of interest in a narrative of pellucid simplicity and from the physical exuberance of play as play, the actor as *player*; mutually interdependent, they are but two sides of the same coin.

The production involves a company drawn from eighteen nationalities. Performers include Andrzej Seweryn and Ryszard Cieslak from Poland (the former known for his work with the influential cinematographer Wajda, the latter the Grotowskian 'holy actor' *par excellence*), Italian film actor Vittorio Mezzogiorno, acclaimed for his central roles in Rosi's *Three Brothers* and Chéreau's *L'Homme blessé*, the Indian screen star and dancer Mallika Sarabhai, as well as the permanent core of Brook's research group. The performance is perhaps above all a hymn to Brook's skill as a director of actors, as an intercultural catalyst. Cultural traditions and differences are cherished as a source of creative friction, not erased in the search for some fallacious theatrical esperanto.

Brook's *Mahabharata* is a dense narrative of immense moral complexity and metaphysical ambiguity, exploring the most profound and timeless of human themes: self-discovery, the forces of moral and personal determination and predestination, man in society and man's destruction of that society. While resolutely refusing any easy answers – politically, psychologically, morally – it constantly gives flesh to a positive attitude in the face of a contradictory plurality of experiences, within which personal and universal are indissolubly intertwined. In performance, parallels with the Western literary tradition (particularly Shakespeare and Homer) abound. However, all is left open, suggested. So, for example, the tragic figure of Dhritarashtra, an old king blind from birth who can only ever hear second-hand reports of the actions of others, comes to life in an astonishing performance by the facially ravaged Cieslak. He saws and spits his way through the text, disinterring echoes of Lear, Gloucester and Oedipus.

In some ways a full reflection and realisation of all Brook's Paris-based research work since 1970, *The Mahabharata* is the most spectacularly conceived of productions, reflecting elements from a variety of popular theatre traditions, as well as Asian dance and martial art forms, and the Chinese circus. Unlocated historically and geographically, like all Brook's work (although Indian culture is visible in many more ways here than, for example, Persia was in *Conference*, a work set on an entirely imaginary plane), the performance is marked by a consciously naïve mixture of styles, traditions, races and accents. Evidence of the journeys to Africa, the Middle East, Asia and even Australia is constantly apparent. The only determinant in this hotch-potch of conventions, some borrowed directly (the Kathakali curtain), others invented and erased in an instant, is effective direct communication.

The performance is essentially the telling of a story by a group of mixed nationality to an assembled ring of spectators. Brook differentiates between the *actor*, who fully inhabits an imaginary character, sinking his own personality in an act of identification and self-transformation, and the *performer*, a Piaf or Garland who only becomes fully charged with life as his/her individuality flowers under the focused spotlight of an audience's attention. He believes one of the most interesting tendencies in contemporary acting to be in the movement towards an amalgamation of the two in the skilled *storyteller* who retains the actor's capacity of transformability, the profundity of his emotional and physical study and understanding, while at the same time remaining freed from the shallow trappings of the actor as naturalistic impersonator. 'Distanced without distancing', the actor is 'transparent', 'invisible', for the role infuses and colours him, not the other way around. Since *Timon* in 1974, Brook has worked to refine this ideal of the actor as storyteller; *The Mahabharata* is its crystalline realisation. Indeed, the whole performance is enacted for the entertainment and edification of an unnamed young boy, almost continuously on-stage. We watch the tale of his ancestors unfold through his eyes, for he is our representative.

As is usual in Brook's work, the decor is deliberately limited throughout. Relationships and locations are established through the geometric positioning of the actors, their play, and their costumes, designed by Chloé Obolensky. These may also serve as simplified guides to character, externalising moral nature or function in the same way as the costumes of the medieval theatre. Brook characteristically chooses to employ single elements (metonymic archetypes as is usual in popular theatre) to concretise the essence of an individual or group. The white robes of the saintly Bhishma alone remain pure and unmarked by the battle, although he has fought at the very epicentre of the carnage. When Karna is made king, a new swathe of elegant silk material is simply placed around his neck. Similarly, when Yudishthira wagers the Pandava kingdoms and property in the game of dice, it is the saffron and white scarves of his brothers and himself that are snatched and lost to the Kauravas. The death of young king is signalled by dipping the corner of a vivid scarlet silk cover in the waters of a river. Some costumes are satirical, darkly comical; reminiscent of the senators in opposition to the Christ-like Timon, the flapping black capes of the Kauravas preparing for battle – suspended at different heights across the back wall – suggest crows. Some of the warriors are virtually sartorial cartoons – breastplates, dressboots, ornate weaponry, samurai bravado and epic gestural presence – but in performance the cartoons come ferociously to life. For example, Bruce Myers' extraordinarily gaunt vocal and physical presence invests the *kshatrya* (warrior) stereotype with a poignant and wretchedly abused humanity to make of Karna, illegitimate half-brother of his sworn enemies and eventual killers, the Pandavas, perhaps the most tragic figure in a tale replete with tragic archetypes. The stereotype is only initial guide, means of social or moral location which can then be undercut or exploded in performance.

Virtually the only objects used throughout (apart from an arsenal of fearsome weaponry) are sticks and bamboo screens: representing bows and arrows, war machines, shields, tents, shelters, beds. Space too is non-specific, virtual, mobile: swathes of Indian material are laid on the bare earth to establish a constantly redefined location. All four elements are omnipresent, active and protean in this most elemental of stories: the beaten red *earth* of the egg-shaped playing space (Mother Earth, source and end of all, and the storyteller's milieu in an Indian village); the free-flowing *water* of a river beside the back wall (life, movement and fertility in Ganga, the river-goddess ancestor of the protagonists) and the enclosed water of a pool (fixed, sterile, a reflective surface to mirror the action, a place for refreshment and ritual ablution, a place to die); candle *flame* as illumination, invocation, purification and creativity, and ball of flame as weapon, injurious to humanity; the *air* that we share with the actors (in Avignon,

22. *The Mahabharata* (1985): The chariot confrontation between Arjuna and Karna; left to right: Arjuna (Vittorio Mezzogiorno, Krishna (Maurice Bénichou), Salya (Tapa Sudana), Karna (Bruce Myers)

the open sky above us). The central chariot confrontation between Arjuna and Karna is a masterpiece of understatement and economy. Their charioteers roll a single wooden cartwheel (the wheel of fortune and *dharma*) before them at high speed, crack whips, mime horses. Eventually the elements conjoin to affect the course of events: suddenly, inexplicably, mud entraps Karna's wheel, holding it fast, rendering him impotent and defenceless. The earth cries out to stop the carnage.

The performance in general is marked by an exacting sense of the visually exciting. A scarlet-faced figure of death, a Kathakali and Kerala martial art (Kalarippayatt) hybrid, dances around the thrusts of an opponent in slow motion, then floats off into darkness with tiny steps, his propulsion apparently generated by the hissing blades of a spring sword he whirls around his head: 'helicopter rotor' or 'electrical force field', as well as unparalleled armament. Arjuna's unwitting confrontation with Shiva, in a clear echo of Chinese opera, is both comic and disturbing: the warrior's arrows are no match for the deity's own prodigious and elemental powers – he manipulates two yellow flags whose movement through the air shatters the silence, like the muffled echo of a distant thunderclap. During the frenzied, stylised battle scenes of *The War*, while actors openly toss handfuls of ochre powder into the air – the dust and smoke of battle – a percussive score improvised by four musicians under the direction of Toshi Tuschitori (placed to one side) underlines the starkly disciplined ensemble manoeuvres and sudden freezes. Our perspective is omnidirectional, continually evolving, as in a film. A number of pyrotechnic images etch themselves into the memory. A small blue tongue of fire snakes its way through the sand in the wake of a celestial nymph, like a comet's tail. A magic circle of flame entraps a group of warriors, forcing them to observe a vision they had invoked (but no longer wish to see) by creating the circle around the pool. In the next scene, charred sand rings the pool in black, like kohl around a glistening eye; it has become a poisoned lake. A torchlit battle–ballet, conducted in growing darkness, culminates in a terrible white explosion, a magnesium flare of positively nuclear dimensions, at the foot of the cliff, as the 'ultimate weapon' is finally unleashed; a pall of acrid smoke engulfs stage and spectators. The work is also one replete with unforgettably violent images of a disarming simplicity. Bhima tears open his enemy's stomach grotesquely, driving his bared teeth into the abdomen; he re-emerges triumphantly blooded with a lacerated elastic red ribbon clenched taut between his teeth. On hearing of the death of his beloved son, the master warrior Drona (Yoshi Oida) abandons the battle to acquiesce passively to death with the silent dignity of a samurai facing *seppuku* (ritual suicide). Subaquatically slowly, he lifts a massive earthenware water-carrier as if to wash the dust and sweat from his lips for the last time. Instead he empties its contents over his head, for it is full of blood; steeped in gore, death is a merciful release.

Brook has arguably reached a culmination of his synthesis of theatre and film techniques in *The Mahabharata*. Like cinematographers, Brook and his actors concentrate our focus of attention on a single individual, a group, a simple telling detail (the close-up), then rapidly expand it outwards to take in the whole (wide/deep focus). In one scene, Arjuna (Vittorio Mezzogiorno) prepares himself to shoot blindfold at a target, like the Zen master in Herrigel's *Zen in the Art of Archery*. The lights dim to a virtual blackout – his blindfold – as he kneels inches from the spectators, taking aim towards the invisible back wall, quietly explaining his actions to us. The moments of immobility and silence as he clears his mind are charged, focused, meditative. At the sudden and mysterious whipping sound of an arrow discharged, full lights shoot up to reveal the entire court assembled in all its glory and pomp: an explosion of sound, colour and light. To cheers and congratulations, Arjuna watches as a bird–kite floats down towards him from an unspecified source at a great height, an arrow lodged in one of its wings; he catches it before it hits the ground. The movement from the privacy and intimacy of intense concentration to grand public spectacle, from 'blindness' to sumptuous sight, is remarkable, for we have shared Arjuna's own perspective, his personal journey. All has been suggested in a conceit of sublime simplicity, which succeeds in transcending the leaden materiality of a deliquescent reality.

A final example comes in the death scene of the 'immortal' warrior Bhishma, on which the outcome of the battle, and by inference the predicament of the universe as a whole, hinges; it is built entirely around the cinematic technique of slow motion. As Arjuna kneels in silence, draws back the imaginary string of his illustrious bow Gandiva and takes aim, all freeze. Krishna, smiling agent of Arjuna's resolve and of *dharma*, plucks the bamboo arrow from the bow and carries it slowly twisting through the air towards Bhishma's heart a few paces away. The suspense in the extension of the instant between life and death is concentrated by the silent immobility of those present and the unearthly enigmatic smile of Krishna, victim of his own prescience. As the arrow strikes home – with child-like gravity Krishna plants it in Bhishma's clothing seconds later – the onlookers erupt in a frenzy of cries and movement, Bhishma collapses mortally wounded, and the baleful drone of the *nagswaram* (an

23. *The Mahabharata*: The death of Bhishma; in the foreground, Arjuna and Sikhandin (Pascaline Pointillart); on the raised platform, Bhishma (Sotigui Kouyate)

anguished cousin of the Western oboe) sings out, like the cry of a wounded elephant. Linear sequential time returns; the narrative pursues relentlessly, renewed.

The Mahabharata has often been seen as a treatise of royal initiation, the making of the king Yudishthira. In many ways, Yudishthira shares the journeys of Turnbull in *The Iks* and Timon into their own 'hearts of darkness', from a philanthropic position of commitment to liberal altruism, through a crisis of enforced lucidity concerning the destructive and materialistic motives of others, to metaphysical pessimism and misanthrophy. Unlike Timon and Turnbull, Yudishthira ultimately refuses self-annihilation in anarchic despair and confusion; like the birds who survive the journey across the desert to the court of their king in *Conference*, he finds a point of transcendent understanding by confronting and assimilating the essence of all aspects of experience, including the 'final illusion' of death: in Brook's terms, a renewal of reintegrated innocence in the fiery rite-of-passage of immersion in experience. *Conference* ended with the birds at the threshold of Paradise; the final image of Brook's *Mahabharata* presents us with a vision of Paradise as a gentle place of music, food, conversation and harmony. The blind can see, the wounded and slaughtered are restored, all animosity is forgotten. The players quietly and without pretence celebrate their collective bringing into life of a resplendent *teatrum mundi*. In Avignon the sense of rebirth was heightened by the timing of the performance to end as the first light of dawn coloured the stone of the quarry: a new day for a new world.

After a lengthy residence at the Bouffes, during which every week the actors will have to perform each part of the trilogy on consecutive days and the continuous 'marathon' version a day later, *The Mahabharata* will be toured around the world for more than two years. An English-language version is in preparation, and talks for a film to be made in India are under way. Eventually (in 1988) it is hoped to take it back to its source, India, to present it in a variety of different environments. It is a production that is sure to go into the annals of theatre history as one of the most significant moments of Brook's extraordinary career, and indeed of contemporary theatre practice. Brook's long-term plans remain uncertain; what more can be achieved with his group after *The Mahabharata*, the fullest crystallisation of theatre as a collaborative undertaking on an immense scale with the richest material he has ever worked on? The energy and imagination of the *enfant terrible* of British theatre in the fifties and sixties, figurehead of European experimental theatre in the seventies, show no signs of flagging. He readily confesses that ultimately his future must lie with the international centre he created:

> In terms of my own life and my own search, the work with the group has shown me that it is possible to make a theatre experience in a purer, simpler, more essential way. I have always searched to make this sort of experience, but the links between the performing group, the content, myself as director and the audience, have never been as organically related as they have been in the Centre. The work in the Centre is organically related to me, and is absolutely central to my own search.[17]

7
Peter Stein

Peter Stein's contribution to directors' theatre is to have clarified the contradictions that inevitably confront a director working within the structure of a collective company today. His distinction is never to have sought to evade these contradictions but rather to have welcomed them. They have emerged in part from our account of other directors, but never so clearly as they appear in the experience of Stein. Schematically, they can be reduced to two fundamental contradictions, one internal and one external to the functioning of the theatre company. The internal contradiction is that of being the *director* within a democratically self-governing *collective*. His company, the Schaubühne, has a complex structure ensuring the maximum participation of each member in decisions of every kind. Yet Stein's working methods are not collaborative in the same sense as Littlewood's or Mnouchkine's. He has always operated on the assumption that 'scenic writing' (the organisation by the director of action and design on stage) is as important as 'dramatic writing' (the playwright's text). He has also seen, however, that it is not sufficient for the director to construct a brilliant production plan. The best results occur when everyone involved has responsibility for artistic decisions and is prepared to call everything into question. Jean Jourdheuil, who has worked as *Dramaturg* with Stein, considers him to be the greatest director of actors alive today. The external contradiction is that of performing *revolutionary* works in a West Berlin theatre heavily subsidised as a showcase for *capitalist* values. Stein's work prompts questions about the relationships between the individual and authority, private satisfactions and the public good. Such questions are not confined to the subject matter of the plays he has produced (such as *The Prince of Homburg* or *Peer Gynt*); they permeate the processes of his work at every level. His role in the German theatre has been not only to question all established practices, but openly to advocate the overthrow of the institutions that pay him. He has been able to do this partly because of the peculiar state of cultural politics in West Berlin and partly because of his own qualities of vision, determination and commitment. One of his exceptional qualities is a sharp awareness of the contradictions involved in his own and his company's work, and his ability to turn this awareness into a significant element of his productions.

The initial impact created by Stein's work on the spectator is best conveyed by the word 'meticulous'. His productions are filled with finely observed detail perfectly timed and presented. Meticulous attention to detail is something he has acknowledged learning from Fritz Kortner, director of the Munich Kammerspiele theatre, where Stein did his first productions. Kortner, who had made his name as an expressionist actor, had been into exile during the Nazi period but had returned to work for the renewal of German theatre after the war. Theatre under the Nazis had been characterised by bombastic productions of the German classics. The tendency to declamation and the fondness for grandiose abstractions so disliked by Brecht had been given full rein. In the post-war period, actors and directors worked to counter these tendencies by reintroducing naturalism or plays on topical themes and by once again introducing important political issues. Nevertheless attempts in this direction were surprisingly tame before the mid 1960s.

In the second half of the decade, things began to change. Piscator, active in political theatre before the war, became director of the Freie Volksbühne in 1963. Here he directed the first productions to establish the new documentary drama: Hochhuth's *The Representative* (1963), Kipphardt's *Robert Oppenheimer* (1964) and Weiss's *The Investigation* (1965). The impact of these productions was tremendous: young theatre workers in Germany were seeing the theatre used for the first time as part of an attempt to confront directly the Nazi past. They began to see that theatre could also be used to make vigorous comments on contemporary social conditions. Stein's choice of Edward Bond's play *Saved* for his first production showed that he intended to follow this path.

Stein had acquired his theatre training by a route more common in Germany's well-subsidised state theatres than elsewhere in the world. After some experiments in student theatre at Munich University, he had persuaded the Munich Kammerspiele to give him freelance work as a *Dramaturg*. This can involve anything from the most menial of tasks to reading and advising on new plays; it gave Stein the entry he needed and enabled him to propose *Saved* for the Kammerspiele's workshop theatre. The play was calculated to create a stir: it had provoked disturbances at London's Royal Court theatre in 1965, even though it was being given as a closed club performance to avoid censorship by the Lord Chamberlain. The success of Stein's 1967 version (named production of the year by the influential journal *Theater heute*) owed a great deal to the decision to translate it not into standard German, but into the Munich dialect. Place names were changed to enable Bond's statement about the bleakness of life for young teenagers in a modern urban landscape to acquire the immediacy of local reference. Although dialect plays are common enough in Munich, the use of dialect is normally reserved for comedies of peasant or working-class life, presented with a degree of sentimentality. Stein's translator, Martin Sperr, was the author of *Hunting Scenes from Lower Bavaria*, a play which had undermined the convention so as to offer an alternative account of ordinary Bavarian life. So the production of *Saved* became part of an attempt to revitalise popular traditions and to use the theatre to reveal unwelcome realities.

In order to achieve this, Stein had to develop a style that was totally authentic in its evocation of the realities facing the young people in the play, but that nevertheless avoided the familiar traps of naturalism: making such a perfect copy of reality that the audience becomes lost in its admiration of the mimesis. His method was similar to that of Brecht – using real objects on stage (a working jukebox, a real rowing boat) but not placing them in illusionistic surroundings: the stage was bare, the back wall illuminated by visible stage lights and the props or scenic elements were brought on by the actors themselves. For his second production at Munich, the first to be designed by Karl-Ernst Herrmann, Stein chose Brecht's early play *In the Jungle of the Cities*. Again it was performed on a bare stage, littered with objects and rubbish suggesting a modern cityscape; in addition, scaffolding was used to construct different levels. Stein added a film sequence of a boxing match at the beginning, and a later sequence of mimed action in which Schlink committed suicide. He also encouraged different styles of acting, the simple directness of Bruno Ganz's performance as Garga contrasting with the heightened gangster style of Pavian and Wurm.[1]

The production confirmed the promise of *Saved* and was invited to the 1986 Berlin Theatre Festival. Stein looked set for a permanent career as a director with the Kammerspiele. But in early 1968 political upheavals were spreading across the continent from France, causing people of left-wing sympathies working in state-funded cultural and educational institutions to reappraise their activity. Stein, in company with a co-director, Wolfgang Schwiedrzik, undertook a production of Peter Weiss's agit-prop *Vietnam Discourse*, designed, rather like Brook's *US*, to express support for the Vietcong and condemnation of American policies in Vietnam. Their staging introduced the satirical singer Wolfgang Neuss as compère and an on-stage audience who drew derisive comments from Neuss. In this way, the production questioned the very function of political theatre in an institution such as the Kammerspiele, where the audience typically contains neither the dominant class of industrialists and property owners nor members of the exploited working class, but only middle-class intellectuals. In order to reinforce the message of the production – that action was required – Neuss proposed to make a collection for the Vietcong at the end of the performance. This was banned by the *Intendant* (administrative director) of the Kammerspiele; Neuss insisted, was sacked, and the two directors resigned in protest. Student disturbances continued well into 1969 and there were further rows and confrontations when Stein's group was invited by Dieter Sturm to perform the *Vietnam Discourse* at the Berlin Schaubühne the following January. In retrospect it is easy to see that the challenge Stein was making was directed less against the Americans (who, after all, were unlikely to be affected) than against the authoritarian management structures then operating in German state theatres. The experience was to lead him to attempt a radical new solution to problems of internal organisation the following year, when he was invited to become a resident director at the Schaubühne.

In the meantime, Stein had helped to draft a proposal, published in *Theater heute* (Dec 1969), for a new form of theatre organisation that would facilitate collective working methods. He was beginning to feel that he could only work as he wanted to if he was part of a permanent ensemble committed to the collective process; he admitted that his company's performances of *Vietnam Discourse* had been part of this elaboration of a method: 'I repeated the production in order to test different kinds of collective work, participation and discussion.'[2]

Yet his work was by no means uniquely concerned with the internal processes of the theatre group. Each of his productions aimed starkly to confront the audience with the contradictions involved in life in a modern capitalist state. For the programme of *Saved*, instead of the usual background material, there was a list of questions for the audience, the collection at the end of *Vietnam Discourse* confronted the audience even more squarely with their own responsibilities: they were made to experience the contradiction involved in applauding a protest play yet doing nothing to change the situation condemned by the play. Here is an example of how Stein embraced the contradictions involved in his work, turning them into the very subject of the performance.

Although it caused a great deal of scandal, agit-prop in
fact took up a comparatively small amount of Stein's
energies at this time, which were mostly spent developing
a working relationship with a group of actors from the
Bremen Theatre and working on his outstanding
production of this period, of Goethe's *Torquato Tasso*,
which opened in Bremen in March 1969. Stein had already
worked as guest director at Bremen in 1967, on a
production of Schiller's *Kabale und Liebe*. Here he had met
the actors Bruno Ganz, Werner Rehm, Edith Clever and
Jutta Lampe, who, with Dieter Lase and Michael König
and the designer Karl-Ernst Herrmann from Munich, were
the nucleus of his ensemble. The outstanding qualities of
this small group of actors and Stein's ability to hold them
together for long enough to build up a genuine ensemble
accounts for much of his success.

Torquato Tasso is a literary play, not at all an obvious
choice for a young political firebrand. It tells the story of
Tasso, court poet at Ferrara towards the end of the
sixteenth century, and of his attempts to maintain a
relationship with his patron, the prince, which can escape
the contingencies of political life. The play shows Goethe at
his most classical, observing the unities and writing
throughout in high-flown verse. He was also clearly
meditating on his own role at the court of Weimar. In his
production Stein decided to emphasise this dual reference.
The costumes suggested eighteenth-century Germany
rather than Renaissance Italy, and a bust of Goethe himself
was placed on stage where Goethe had called for busts of
Ariosto and Virgil. The stage, mostly bare, was covered by
a luxurious green carpet and surrounded by perspex
screens, the whole suggesting opulence of a rather modern
kind. In this way the production suggested not only Goethe
looking back to classical models and contrasting them with

his own role, but also Stein looking back to Goethe, meditating on the role of the artist in modern society.

The interpretation of Stein's production was thus multi-layered, but also quite clear. It suggested that the artist who fondly believes that his art gives him a privileged position in society, or puts him outside normal political exigencies, is fooling himself. The final image of the play, a typically daring conception, expressed this very clearly:

> After Tasso's famous concluding speech comparing himself to a shipwrecked mariner clinging to the rock of Antonio, Ganz clambered up onto Werner Rehm's shoulder. He squatted there, looking back over Rehm's head with the mindless complacency of a monkey who has just neatly completed its turn and is being carried off by its trainer.[3]

Stein's work in 1968–9 was entirely typical in its general approach of what he was to achieve at the Schaubühne in the 1970s. He had succeeded in producing three very different plays, by Goethe, Brecht and Weiss, in such a way as to bring out from each its relevance to the problem of art and its importance to effect social change. In doing so, he had demonstrated his mastery of 'scenic writing' – in other words, his production deliberately sought to add a whole new dimension of meaning to the playwright's original text. This was evident in the additional sequences or characters that Stein introduced to the plays by Brecht and Weiss, but it was particularly clear in his treatment of *Torquato Tasso*, which involved major adaptations of Goethe's text. About a quarter of the play was cut, particularly the lines emphasising Tasso's poetic skill; Tasso's speeches were cut more heavily than those of the prince. A prologue was added, in which each character presented him- or herself to the audience with isolated statements drawn from various points in the play's first two acts and brutally juxtaposed with no attempt to re-create Goethe's smooth exposition. The play was then broken up into ten episodes and two 'interludes', following the order of events in Goethe's plot, but interrupting its flow and giving each episode a title in the style of Brecht. The idea was to increase the audience's ability to react critically to the performance. The acting style was similarly inspired by Brechtian theory, seeking to offer the character's words not as carrying simple conviction, but as statements to be weighed up and judged.

For the 1969–70 season, Stein and his fledgling ensemble were invited to work in Zurich. Their productions reflected a similar mix to those of the previous year: Bond's *Early Morning*; O'Casey's *Cock-a-doodle Dandy*, and Middleton and Rowley's *The Changeling*. For the adaptation of the last, Stein invited Dieter Sturm to join him, and this was the beginning of a fruitful collaboration. However, the style of Stein's three productions was too harsh for those in control of the Zurich theatre, and so Stein accepted an offer from the Berlin Senate to move to West Berlin. The Schaubühne am Halleschen Ufer agreed to house the company, which after some hard bargaining was allotted an annual subsidy of DM1.8 million, in return for which it had to mount at least four productions a year and give at least 250 performances. One consequence of this move was financial security for the company. The subsidy grew regularly, reaching DM17 million in 1983, with the result that the financial pressures under which so many directors have had to labour were never a problem for Stein. Furthermore, they have been able to reconstruct a building (the Mendelssohn-Bau on the Lehninplatz) entirely according to their needs. This new theatre offers the utmost flexibility: at least twelve different configurations of the stage and auditorium spaces. Even before the company moved in, in 1981, it had been able to experiment with different playing spaces. *Shakespeare's Memory* and *As You Like It* were performed in film studios at Spandau. The generosity of the West Berlin authorities is explained by their need to promote Berlin as a centre of free cultural enterprise, and the Stein company has certainly proved a good investment in this respect. Stein, characteristically, has refused to countenance the accusation that he is living off 'dirty' money. He commented to Bernard Dort that, if the West Berliners were determined to throw away their money, it was better to throw it away on theatre than on yet another Starfighter.

Stein explained to Dort that he welcomed the Berlin offer mainly because it allowed him a rare opportunity to experiment with an ideal theatre organisation: 'We wished to set up an organisation which would be a model (as well as an experiment) allowing different groups and different sectors within the same company to take autonomous decisions and enabling general decisions, at the highest level, to result from common agreement of all concerned.' The establishment of such a structure served several purposes, not merely that of facilitating ensemble work. It allowed political ideas to be tested at a manageable level – that of the company's own internal relationships; Stein was always more interested in practice than in theory. It also allowed for each member of the company to find personal fulfilment in the work: 'Everybody is able to create something, to work towards a complex production and to make a significant contribution.'[4]

If the organisation set up to achieve this was in some ways less communal than that of Theatre Workshop or of the first Théâtre du Soleil, it was none the less carefully structured, and that structure was more explicit. The key to the organisation was the *Vollversammlung* or general meeting, which had final responsibility for all decisions. Meeting at first once a month, this body could veto any decision taken by the directorial committee, which consisted of the two licencees of the theatre, who were permanent members, and three elected members. As a director, Stein was eligible for election but no more eligible than any other company member; he was not always on it. The committee held open meetings twice a week at which anyone was free to voice an opinion. A standing sub-committee acted as a link between the directorial committee and the separate committees of production staff, actors, technicians and administrators. There was also a separate committee for appointments. Each of these committees issued minutes of their meetings, which were circulated to everyone in the company. Equality of salaries was not introduced, but the differentials were far less extreme than in most German theatres.

The successes and failures of this attempt at a structure for collective responsibility have been set out by Michael Patterson. It was evidently a structure within which not every director felt at ease: Klaus Peymann, a founder member of the company and a co-author with Stein of the 1969 participation plan published in *Theater heute*, left after the first year, whereas Klaus-Michael Grüber, who was invited to join in 1971 and directed his first production in 1972, has stayed. Other guest directors have found the questioning, anti-authoritarian attitudes of the actors too much to take. Stein's success with the group appears to depend on his total commitment to the collective process, even when it works to his own inconvenience, and his ability to command the loyalty of first-rate actors. In these contradictory qualities he partly resembles both Joan Littlewood and Ariane Mnouchkine. Like them, his insistence that he is not the centre of creativity, but that all carry an equal responsibility, paradoxically reinforces his authority with the actors.

From the outset, Stein's working methods involved a strong emphasis on research or discovery by all members of the company, and this covered both the internal organisation of the group and the object of their work. In order to raise the general level of political consciousness and to inform the managerial discussions within the group, political seminars were arranged, which everyone attended in working hours. The subjects studied were *The Communist Manifesto* and the writings of Lenin. But the whole purpose and function of the company's production work was also defined in terms of a learning experience. When Stein was asked by Dort in 1972 about the plans he had for the repertoire when setting up the Schaubühne, his response was to suggest that the company wanted to work along two broad lines:

> We wanted to concern ourselves with subjects not normally dealt with in the theatre, that is to say the history of revolution or revolutions and of the working class movement. That was our firm intention. And we were conscious of everything that implied: raising our political consciousness, studying the historical facts, etc. In short our need to learn, not only about aesthetic matters, but also and especially about historical matters. That can only be a long-term undertaking. The other direction concerned the past and the history of the bourgeois class. There again, it seemed important to us to know more about it and to deal with it in our productions.[5]

The intriguing and unusual thing about this as a declaration of intent is its emphasis on what is to be to *learnt* rather than what is to be to *shown*. We shall see that this intention to treat work at the Schaubühne as a journey of discovery was fully borne out in the subsequent history of the company. Of the two different directions identified by Stein, the first appeared predominant in the early years of the Schaubühne. The first performances put on by the new company were of *Torquato Tasso*, but the first new production was of *The Mother*. This play was written in 1931 by Brecht, adapting Gorki's story of 1907 about how a working-class woman, who started out opposing the revolution, came to identify with its aims and to work for its success. At first the rehearsals were attended by every actor in the company; anyone was free to question or comment at the conclusion of each rehearsal. More importantly, work on the play included a mass of research, in which all took part, into the history of revolutionary movements in Russia and Germany. Therese Giehse, who had worked with Brecht before the war, was invited to play the part of the Mother; through her presence the company enjoyed a living link not just with revolutionary movements of the 1920s but also with revolutionary theatre practice. Rehearsals continued for an intense two-month period and the play opened on 8 October 1970. The word used by Peter Iden to sum up the quality of the performance was 'Clarity – that is the beauty of this production. And here clarity also means correct and considered application of the theatrical means employed.'[6] The theatrical means consisted of a thrust stage with the audience on three sides and the cast sitting on the fourth, present throughout the performance and helping with scene changes. As Brecht had recommended (and as in the case of *Torquato Tasso*) the stage was permanently bathed in brilliant white light. There was a panel above the stage for captions and two screens on either side for projections. The acting style was also as Brecht had demanded: intensely real, with meticulous attention to detail of gesture, movement and grouping, but without attempting to create the illusion of identity between actors and characters: the actors were clearly demonstrating a sequence of situations, telling a story. Jack Zipes expressed the quality of the acting as follows:

Two styles of acting were evolved. The actors playing the young revolutionaries were characterized by a simplicity and directness in their gestures and the manner in which they worked cooperatively. The bourgeois characters such as the Czarist police chief, the teacher and the landlord used pomp, exaggeration and deceit to show their egocentricity and lack of social consciousness. Both Pelegea Vlassova (the Mother) and the teacher changed their individualistic styles in the course of the play to correspond to that of the revolutionaries. Their individualities did not become lost in the collective but became more humane. It was this learning process of change which became the central theme of the Schaubühne production – a change of views and action. It was not so much the conflict between bourgeois and proletarian classes which the Schaubühne emphasized but the alternative to a life style which is perceived as self-defeating, artificial and oppressive. The bearing of the actors toward the audience was not preachy or doctrinaire. Rather, the actors tried to make their own learning process available to spectators through the straightforward, friendly narrative manner in which they explained and demonstrated events on the stage.[7]

This description provides a very clear picture of the

importance of the learning process in the production and how it was successfully exteriorised in performance. Work along the same lines continued with Vishnevsky's *The Optimistic Tragedy* in 1972. In the meantime, Stein had also directed two plays for performances specifically aimed at workers and apprentices: Enzensberger's *The Havana Hearing* and Kelling's *The Altercation*, both documentary dramas performed with the primary aim of raising political consciousness amongst workers. They were performed mostly in youth clubs, largely because the trades unions took exception to the criticism of a shop steward in *The Altercation*, refusing to allow it to be shown on their premises. Fairly quickly, the company came to the conclusion that agit-prop work was better left to the workers themselves and, moreover, that it was not what the company could do best. The last portable performance of this kind put on by the company was a documentary about workers' revolts in 1921, constructed by Wolfgang Schwiedrzik. Schwiedrzik criticised what he saw as a blunting of the company's political edge and left in 1975.

The evolution in Stein's attitude towards political theatre can be seen most clearly in a comment he made to Bernard Dort about a planned show on the Paris Commune which was never completed. He explained that he had rejected both the existing plays on the subject by Brecht and Adamov, and had sketched out a possible show in which the subject was to be 'the end of the bourgeois conception of revolution and the emergence of a different form of revolution, a different aesthetic, a different mode of representation and different metaphors for revolution since the Commune. That, I believe, is an interesting subject for the theatre'.[8] This shows Stein's continuing interest in developing the language of theatre, aware that its prime function is not to preach but to perform. His ideas about the bourgeois conception of revolution were used in a later production of *La Cagnotte* (*The Pig-Bank*) by Labiche.

The second direction identified by Stein (the history of the bourgeois class) was pursued through performances of Ibsen's *Peer Gynt* (1971), Kleist's *The Prince of Homburg* (1972), Labiche's *The Pig-Bank* (1973), Handke's *They Are Dying Out* (1974) and Gorki's *Summerfolk* (1974). New versions were made for several of these plays, especially *The Pig-Bank*, which was adapted and translated with the help of two *Dramaturgen*, Botho Strauss and Jean Jourdheuil. An intensely pragmatic director, Stein does not approach directing with a ready-made system. Each of the above plays presents particular problems of dramaturgy and production. For each one, Stein and his team elaborated a different set of solutions: different spatial arrangements, different uses of scenery, costumes and masks, different acting styles, positioning, grouping and pacing. Each was the subject of massive research (some of which was made available in printed form in the lavish programmes) and it is impossible to do them justice in an account of this kind. Two contrasting examples, *Peer Gynt* and *Summerfolk*, will enable us to identify the qualities of Stein's directing work; detailed discussion of these productions will be found in Michael Patterson's book.

Although Stein rejects ready-made systems, his working method remains similar from one production to the next. The key to this method is that, unlike directors such as Planchon or Strehler, he does not come to the first rehearsals with a prepared *mise en scène*, but elaborates the production ideas, the design, even the adaptation, in the course of working on the play with the actors. Over the years he has come to rely more and more on this method, which explains the harsh comments he now makes on his early productions. In 1983 he condemned his production of *Torquato Tasso* as simply using Goethe's play to make simplistic statements; he claimed that the film version made him ready to die of shame. Here he was condemning the tendency of directors to approach production with fixed ideas. He also criticised *Peer Gynt*, but not for the same reason: 'In *Peer Gynt* the actors messed about shamelessly. There was no genuine work on the part of the actors. As a result a sort of impudence was apparent, a superficiality in the concretization of the structures of the play, which I could no longer bear'.[9] Like many artists, Stein is particularly harsh on his own work, and this criticism is made from the standpoint of his belief that the work of production should bring out the complexities and multiple meanings of a play, rather than make a univocal statement. But in 1971 he was as interested in discovering and representing the nineteenth-century bourgeois view of the individual as he was in being true to Ibsen's play.

Peer Gynt is a long play, whose meaning can only be fully grasped in its very length. We have to see Peer's youthful ebullience giving way to self-seeking, lechery, greed in the course of his travels around the world. We have to follow his mythical quest for fame and fortune in far-off lands. We have to experience the aging process and then watch Peer return to his beginnings still unsatisfied in his quest for self-fulfilment. Whole episodes of the play are frequently cut to reduce it to a length that can be performed in one evening, but, because the effect of the play is cumulative, any such cuts involve changing the meaning of the whole. The decision was taken to perform the play in its entirety over two evenings.

The Schaubühne auditorium was adapted to establish a particular relationship between the audience and the action. The playing space ran the length of the theatre, using both ends and the middle ground, while the audience seating was arranged on either side, with the two audience blocks facing one another across the middle ground. This made it possible for the audience to be drawn closely into Peer's adventures, but it also gave spatial expression to the theme of the journey, since Peer was seen to move across a considerable distance and different parts of the set opened unexpectedly to reveal further locations: the troll king's hall was revealed under the hillside at one end; the Sphinx was winched up out of the floor to reveal a lunatic asylum. Paradoxically, this actor–audience arrangement also made it possible to set the action at an ironic distance from the audience by showing two things simultaneously. For example, in much of the fourth and fifth acts Solveig could

24. *Peer Gynt* (1971): The Sphinx; note audience sitting on either side of rectangular acting space; design by Karl-Ernst Herrmann

be seen by her hut, growing old as she waited for Peer's return.

A further difficulty facing theatre directors in deciding how to stage the play is the sheer size of the role of Peer. This problem was solved in characteristic fashion by dividing the role between six actors. Apart from making it easier to show Peer aging, this arrangement contributed to the Marxist interpretation of the role, stressing the discontinuities in a character whose consciousness is changed and formed by his changing environment. But Marxist demystification was not allowed to destroy the fabulous aspects of Peer's adventures. In particular the trolls were extraordinarily impressive. Too often, this part of the play fails to carry conviction, since the trolls are made to look like overgrown garden gnomes. Stein understood that the trolls had to be seen as a concrete image for respectable Victorian society's fear of the bestiality that it secretly condoned or even cultivated. In Stein's production, costumes and masks were elaborated to suggest both bourgeois desire for respectability and the grotesque distortions of vice. The aim was for the troll figures to present a distorted nightmarish mirroring of the society of Haegstad. Taken as a whole, Stein's production work was a triumph of inventive 'scenic writing', controlled by strict fidelity to Ibsen's guiding idea. Peer represents the urge to egocentric self-fulfilment upon which capitalism depends for its justification. Ibsen expressed this largely in poetic terms; Stein added images to fill out the social and political context and the historical perspective of the years that had elapsed since the play was written.

The production of *Summerfolk* fitted with both the exploration of the history of revolution and with that of the bourgeoisie. Gorki's play, written in 1904, has some similarities with Chekhov's *Seagull*; it shows a group of

25.   *Summerfolk* (1974): Design by Karl-Ernst Herrmann

professional people who have left their normal city life to spend the summer in the country. Like Chekhov's play, it presents this class of people as futile and inward-looking; as in Chekhov, they have long aimless discussions and play at amateur dramatics. But Gorki takes an attitude that is both harsher and more positive: some of his characters are more thoroughly unpleasant than Chekhov's; others finally break through to an optimistic conclusion. Gorki is clear both in his condemnation of the failings of the bourgeoisie and in his conviction that a working-class revolution would clear them away and substitute a better social order.

As in the case of other productions, the preparations for this one involved thorough background research, including a journey to Russia by the whole cast. It also involved, for the first time in the company's existence, work on

Stanislavski and on acting techniques designed to create intense psychological realism. In the course of this preparatory work, the idea was conceived of having all the characters on stage throughout. This allowed the company to capitalise on one of its main strengths: the quality of its ensemble work. It also meant that, as with *The Mother*, there was complete continuity between the work *process* and the final *product*. The performance showed the actors once again making their own learning process available to the spectators in a style that was fascinating to watch for its combination of detail and clarity. Furthermore, the presence of all the main actors on stage served to retain an emphasis on a social group rather than on particular individuals. The audience was acutely conscious of watching a whole class whose failure was collective, not merely a set of failed individuals.

This impression was underlined by Karl-Ernst Herrmann's extraordinary setting. The front part of the stage was used as if it were the veranda of the holiday house. At the back, and to right and left, a dense forest of birch trees closed off the perspective on all sides so that spectators had a powerful sense of the actors being enclosed by a cage: real trees planted in real earth and carefully watered before each performance, their very reality contributed to the sense of intolerable claustrophobia. Beyond the trees, peasants and nightwatchmen periodically passed, commenting on the antics of the holidaymakers or banging sticks against the treetrunks to warn off possible intruders. One of Stein's first ideas had been for a promenade production in a garden, with the audience moving from one group of actors to the next. By concentrating all the characters in one space and keeping them all visible throughout, he created a strong concrete image of their inability to escape from one

26. *Summerfolk*: The birch forest

another until the end, when Maria Lvovna does succeed in breaking out, persuading four others to accompany her.

Once again Stein had understood and embraced the contradictions of his own working practice: the naturalist performance style, originally elaborated in order to elevate the concerns and the history of the middle classes to the level of serious significant action once reserved for tragedy, was here being turned against that very class. In other words, the meticulous construction of character and environment through concentration on totally realistic, imitative performance was so perfect that it stood clearly revealed as a kind of fetishistic navel-gazing. The trees were too real and too many, the characters too convincing and too relentlessly present, so that the whole performance induced in its audience an overpowering desire to run, to escape, to utterly reject these pompous, silly, egocentric people and the world they had created in their own image. The performance style which had been created to dignify them succeeded only in showing up mercilessly, as if under a microscope, the pettiness of their behaviour.

In order to make it possible for all the characters to be on stage, considerable rewriting was needed, especially of the first two acts. As in previous productions, Stein and Strauss were happy to do this, showing no compunction about subordinating Gorki's text to the demands of performance; indeed their adaptation became a new text with an afterlife of its own, being translated into French and performed in 1976 by the Comédie de Caen. For Stein, as for Planchon, the importance of the scenic writing was at least as great as that of the dramatic writing. In *Summerfolk* he reversed the usual order of precedence, since the text was adjusted to fit the chosen performance style, not the performance to fit the text. Patterson further suggests that Stein should be seen as almost the co-author of Botho Strauss's plays – at least, those that he has directed: *Trilogie des Wiedersehens*, *Gross and Klein* and *Der Park*.

The culminating example of Stein's particular approach to directing came in 1976 and 1977 with his work on Shakespeare. The company devoted two years to this project, in the course of which their emphasis on research and exploring new skills was pushed to its limit. For the first year they combined academic research on Elizabethan views of society, philosophy, religion and science with training in practical skills such as singing Elizabethan music, playing Elizabethan instruments, learning contemporary forms of dancing, acrobatics, and so forth. Such a wealth of materials was accumulated that the company decided that Stein should structure them into a public show and this was presented over two evenings in a film studio at Spandau, opening in December 1976. It was mostly arranged as a promenade performance with several competing centres of interest and the audience free to move around. The exhibits included extracts from folk plays, from the work of Shakespeare's contemporaries, pageant wagons, demonstrations of medicine, astrology, seafaring and ship-building. The English title, *Shakespeare's Memory*, was intended to bring out a double emphasis in this unusual show: both a re-creation of Shakespeare's world for the twentieth-century public, and an attempt to demonstrate Shakespeare's own view of history. Beneath it all lay the conviction, shared by Planchon, that Shakespeare's modernity lies in his awareness of living at a time of transition: no longer at ease with the medieval world-view, yet conscious of being only on the brink of a new age whose structures were not yet established. Stein was always searching in his productions to transcend the normal, rather rigid structure of actor–audience relationships, so as to create the conditions for a genuine exchange between performers and spectators. In *Shakespeare's Memory*, he felt he had succeeded:

The significant element in this project is its openness with the audience and with one another. We dare to share our preferences and personal passions, and we receive wonderful gifts from the public – it's a real exchange. The discussions that follow each performance are more successful than we ever planned.[10]

This preparatory work found its proper conclusion in the remarkable production of *As You Like It*, also given at the Spandau studio, in September 1977. The fundamental principle of a variable spatial relation between action and audience was retained in the following manner:

27. *As You Like It* (1977): Design by Karl-Ernst Herrmann

Shakespeare's scene order was rearranged, so as to group all the episodes at the court of Duke Frederick in the first part of the play. This was performed in a large hall (as it might have been in the great hall of some Elizabethan manor house) with raised stages round the edge and the audience standing in the middle. The lighting was largely from beneath and the colours were hard blues and whites. There were no signs of wealth or luxury except in the very rich, dark-coloured costumes. The performances, however, gave an impression of extreme tension and smouldering physicality which heightened the sense of the court as a place of danger and repressed desire. This physicality was underlined by the staging of the wrestling match, for which a professional wrestler was hired to take the part of Charles, his lines being redistributed. Orlando (Michael König) stripped to a loincloth and the fight was played out as a fine display of licensed physical aggression.

28.   *As You Like It*: The wrestling match

For the second part of the play, in the Forest of Arden, the audience filed, one by one, through a narrow tunnel whose walls dripped water to emerge, as if reborn, into a vast open space evoking an idyllic Arden. There was a sizable pool, a field of standing corn, an enormous beech tree and a peasant farmstead. The picture was not over-romanticised: the harsh realities of peasant existence were given their due weight, but Shakespeare's essential structural contrast between the two differing worlds of the court and the Forest of Arden emerged with extraordinary force and clarity. For this part, the audience were seated, the action taking place above, below and around them.

The performances which Stein drew from his actors in this section of the play were quite outstanding. The broad method was the same as that employed in *Summerfolk*: all the actors were on-stage all the time and their activities continued even when they were not the focus of the action or the dialogue. But, despite the multiple activities of total environment built up by Stein and his designer Herrmann, there were also moments of great stillness and concentration – as, for example, in some of the early scenes between Rosalind (Jutta Lampe) and Celia (Tina Engel), who managed to convey a mutual dependence almost physical in its intensity and extraordinarily moving. The research of the previous year was used on many occasions, one example being the stag dance, for which the actors drew on their study of folk plays and dances. This became a scene of great power, in which actors re-created the hunt and mimed the killing of the deer. At this point, as Patterson wrote,

> The lights dimmed eerily and Rosalind and Celia fell asleep in each others arms. Orlando could be observed painting his face like a woman and caressing his breasts.

The figure draped with the deerskin then confronted Orlando and they became locked in a violent struggle, while Rosalind and Celia rolled across the ground in a tight embrace.[11]

The wooing scenes between Rosalind and Orlando were performed with great intensity, almost as if they were in a dream, and the singing of 'It was a lover and his lass' was accompanied by a kind of ring dance which culminated in Audrey being bodily lifted and placed on top of Touchstone. In all of these ways, a tension was created as powerful as that evoked in the first half; but, instead of being associated with repression and power, here it was associated with liberation and the stirrings of erotic passion not fully understood by the protagonists themselves. By playing at being someone else, Rosalind was slowly becoming a different person – an interpretation of her role which took its place naturally in the preoccupation with the process of enactment that runs through almost all Stein's productions.

The force of the pastoral environment took on a particular power and attraction for the West Berlin audience, for whom easy escape to the country is almost impossible. Stein used the basic conflict between aggressive city (or court) life and enveloping pastoral life to create some of his most memorable effects. One of these occurred near the end of the performance, with the arrival of Duke Frederick's army (only threatened in Shakespeare's original). Here they broke violently through the undergrowth but suddenly slowed down and sank, as if overcome by magic, onto the floor of the forest; at the same time their armour almost literally fell from them and they were transformed by the power of the natural world. To close the performance, a pageant wagon representing

29. *As You Like It*: The forest of Arden; Phebe (Elke Petri)

Hymen rolled on and the various couples took their places on it to return to court. Only melancholy Jaques refused to join them and remained behind. The lasting impression was of an idyllic utopia constantly undermined and challenged but constantly beckoning, holding out hopes of renewal. The programme quoted from Jan Kott's analysis in *Shakespeare our Contemporary*: 'Shakespeare takes us into the Forest of Arden in order to show that one must try to escape, although there is no escape; that the Forest of Arden does not exist, but those who do not run away will be murdered.'

After the work on Shakespeare, Stein undertook two more large-scale projects, Botho Strauss's *Trilogie des Wiedersehens* and Aeschylus's Oresteian trilogy. Both were highly praised for meticulous staging and fine performances. In them, Stein showed his versatility, moving with ease from plays about contemporary life to one of the oldest tragedies in the Western tradition.

The *Oresteia* can be seen as the first example of a new faithfulness to authorial text that was to become a feature of Stein's work in the 1980s. Stein and his *Dramaturg* (Marleen Stössel for this production) made a new translation aiming at maximum simplicity and faithfulness to the text. They also produced a 400-page document about the history of Athens and of the Ancient Greek theatre and including a detailed critical examination of the trilogy. The staging too aimed for faithfulness to Greek theatre practice: the audience sat on tiered benches arranged in the shape of an amphitheatre; there was a large *orchestra* or dancing space; and the stage was bare except for the statue of a Greek warrior. At the back of the stage was a wall, a door and an *ekkyklema* (small platform for displaying bodies), which was thrust forward at the appropriate moment. Agamemnon's chariot ran down-stage on rails laid by the chorus, who were masked. Neither chariot nor masks were imitations of their Greek equivalents, but the qualities of the production lay in its acceptance of the limitations of Ancient Greek theatre practice, particularly evident in the immensely powerful chorus passages.

Similar qualities were particularly apparent in Stein's much-acclaimed 1983 production of Genet's play *The Blacks*. Genet's plays present the director with an unusual challenge since they are more ceremonies than stories, while retaining a close link to political realities. *The Blacks* is in some ways the most difficult of all, since Genet insists that the play must be performed only by black actors and only in front of a white audience. This is because it dramatises not a story but a struggle between two languages, two sets of cultural associations and value systems. By imposing their language on the colonised people, the colonisers have forced the natives to adopt all the hidden value judgements enshrined in the French language. In Genet's play a group of blacks face a white court, also played by blacks, wearing white masks. Beneath their horrified gaze, the blacks enact the rape and murder of a white woman. The court appeals to Racinean purity, metaphoric whiteness, the white man's civilising mission; the blacks respond with a 'litany of the livid' exploiting the unpleasant associations of pallor, then develop a new set of value associations in which black acquires positive connotations. Genet prescribes the precise details of this ritual: the movements, the music, the use of masks, costumes and props. For example, he specifies a raised gallery running round the back of the stage from which the court looks down on the action, so that the negroes' ceremony is caught between the facing ranks of white audience and white court: the gaze of the one is reflected in the gaze of the other. He also specifies that the play

30. *The Blacks* (1983): Fireworks announce the execution of a traitor offstage; design by Karl-Ernst Herrmann

opens with the negroes dancing a minuet to a tune by Mozart.

In Stein's production these and other stage directions were scrupulously followed. Unlike in earlier plays he had worked on, nothing was changed. All Stein's ingenuity was turned to giving a faithful production, and there were some brilliant touches. The Mozart minuet, for example, was hummed by the blacks as they danced in perfect harmony. The masks of the white court were supplemented by hundreds of other white masks which descended from the flies as Village insisted that he loved Vertu – a mass of voyeurs gloating in their power over the blacks. For in Genet's ceremony the blacks have to refuse love as something polluted by the way in which it has been annexed by white civilisation. Instead their only hope is in cultivating hatred, and the difficulty of this was demonstrated with great clarity as Village and Vertu tried to develop a verbal language of hatred while all their body language expressed desire for one another.

This is just one example of the outstanding intelligence that Stein brought to the production. Everything made sense, everything fell into place, and the spectator's satisfaction was that of seeing the author's intentions meticulously and brilliantly followed. Paradoxically, this too explains the limitations of this production, which, for all its energetic commitment, somehow lacked emotional conviction and failed to move. For Stein, working with his ensemble, simply could not respect Genet's fundamental insistence that the play should be performed by blacks.

Discussing *The Blacks*, Stein stressed the fact that the choice of play fitted with the way the Schaubühne had always worked:

> We chose *Les Nègres* because it opened up a subject having to do with the activity of theatre and one which we thought we could usefully explore and learn from. The subject was Africa, the European–African relationship, of course, as the play describes it. Moreover the actors were keen to work as a chorus and they are all on stage all the time as in the *Oresteia*: we wanted to pursue that.[12]

He added that the play also fitted with the group's continuing desire to follow up experiences not normally available to actors – in this case getting to know Africa. They made a brief trip to Africa, where they learned some basic African dance steps, and these were put to good effect in the performance, though the women were markedly

31. *The Blacks*: Stein's added ending

better at it than the men. Stein made one addition (the only one) to the end of the play. After the final return of the Mozart minuet, a huge map of Africa appeared on the back wall, with the independent countries coloured in red, while Mozart gave way to drumming and an ecstatic African dance.

It is clear from this that the aim of the production was no different from that behind many earlier productions: it was to learn, to grow, both politically and as actors. Genet's play appealed both because of its political stance and because of its theatrical sophistication. Many reviewers complained that the Schaubühne had misunderstood

Genet's play. For example, Michael Stone in *The Guardian*
(24 June 1983) wrote that 'Genet did not really write a play
about racial discrimination and its effects on its victims.
The Blacks is only another expression of Genet's anarchist
love of Mayhem.' This is certainly mistaken. The constant
references in the play to a real political murder supposedly
taking place off-stage remind the audience that, although
actors can only deal with images, others elsewhere deal in
flesh-and-blood realities. Ville de Saint-Nazaire is the
concrete link to this 'elsewhere'. The mistake of the
Schaubühne was not to hint at a political dimension but to
overlook the play's main political thrust, which consists in
showing blacks defying and destroying whites. For blacks
to accept the image of whites and then distort, change,
explode that image, they need to start as real blacks. The
additional alienation effect provided by having whites
black up in the first place simply undermines the power of
the underlying confrontation. Miriam Goldschmidt, as the
only black actress, brought the role of Félicité a note of
power and authenticity that was lacking from the other
interpretations, even that of Christiane Petersen, who, as
Bobo, filled the stage with restless movement.

Even more successful with the Schaubühne's Berlin
public was Stein's *Three Sisters*, first performed in 1984.
The resources of the new theatre enabled the company to
perform in sets of astonishing realism, both interior and
exterior, and their ensemble playing was, once again,
remarkable. Karl-Ernst Herrmann exploited all three
performance areas to create a set that was seen by some
critics as perfection itself. Others felt that Stein had
sacrificed too much in order to achieve the perfect
naturalistic illusion of reality. They pointed out that, in
earlier productions, such as *Summerfolk* and *Peer Gynt*,
Stein's concern had been not merely to reproduce, but also

to comment on, the world of the nineteenth-century bourgeoisie. Audiences seemed to worry less about these distinctions: they went to be impressed and moved and they came away satisfied. *Theater heute* named *The Three Sisters* production of the year (as it had done for *Saved* in 1967) and the production became one of the company's biggest commercial hits.

Why then did Stein resign his post as artistic director of the Schaubühne in 1985? He possessed a perfectly flexible

32.   *Three Sisters* (1984): Act I; design by Karl-Ernst Herrmann; left to right: Masha (Jutta Lampe), Vershinin (Otto Sander), Olga (Edith Clever), Kulyigin (Werner Rehm), Solyony (Roland Schäfer), Rodé (Nicolaus Dutsch), Irina (Corinna Kirchhoff), Tuzenbach (Ernst Stotzner), Fedotik (Jochen Torote), Natasha (Tina Engel), Andrej (Peter Simonischek), Chebutykin (Wolf Redl)

33.   *Three Sisters*: Act IV

theatre building, an ensemble of outstanding actors who had worked together for nearly two decades, and a virtually limitless budget. It seems likely that both he and his ensemble felt that they had reached the end of their abilities to produce work that was new and challenging. This was reinforced by the nature of the Schaubühne's audience: Stein's attempts at theatre for workers and apprentices had failed; his productions tracing the history of the bourgeoisie had succeeded magnificently, but they had become a snob success. Attendance at Schaubühne productions had become a 'must' for the upper echelons of West Berlin society. When Stein had turned towards the Third World with *The Blacks*, his production had lacked political thrust. In short, he appeared to be imprisoned in his culture palace.

Whatever Stein's private reasons for leaving his permanent post at the Schaubühne, it is clear that the contradictions which fuelled his work at the outset had become blunted with time. The creative struggles to define his role within the ensemble had been more or less resolved. Moreover, his attempts to give a questioning, even a revolutionary, edge to his productions of the classics seem to have diminished in proportion to his growing success with the Berlin bourgeoisie. His choice of new plays to direct during the period 1978–84 certainly reveals a diminution of the fiery optimism apparent during the early 1970s. Botho Strauss's *Trilogie des Wiedersehens* and *Gross und Klein* and Nigel Williams' *Class Enemy* are bleak chronicles of the forces of barbarism in our contemporary urban culture. This shift was painfully obvious in the adaptation by Botho Strauss of *A Midsummer Night's Dream: Der Park*, directed by Stein in 1984. The forest scenes contained none of the erotic power or idyllic quality of Arden in the 1977 *As You Like It*. Instead the play was set in a littered, polluted park more reminiscent of *Saved*, and the characters were all products of a violent and alienating environment.

Stein did not entirely sever links with the Schaubühne, arranging to return for regular guest productions. The first of these, Eugene O'Neill's *The Hairy Ape* (1986), was an international success, demonstrating that he had not lost his talent for directing ensemble work of outstanding quality. In 1986 he also launched into opera with a highly praised *Otello* for the Welsh National Opera, using the strength of that company's chorus to reinterpret Verdi's music drama as the enactment of Otello's relationship with his people as much as with his wife. But Stein's work with the Schaubühne during the early 1970s had resulted in something more than fine productions: like Brecht before him, Stein had showed how a director of genius can mobilise the energies of an ensemble so as to change the way a whole society understands itself.

8
Robert Wilson

Robert Wilson is the supreme example of director as scenic writer. He draws on a wide variety of artistic sources, from symbolism to the visionary architecture of the late twentieth century, from surrealist dream imagery to post-modern choreography and the perceptual modes of so-called 'maladjusted' children. He is unique in his uncompromising fidelity to the realisation of his own visions in performance, fuelled by a quasi-mystical belief in the therapeutic power of art as a stimulus to the individual imagination. He takes his place in the tradition of visionary mystics and romantic innovators of the last 150 years that has its origins in the 'music drama' of Richard Wagner and subsequently in the theories of Edward Gordon Craig. Wagner's principle theoretical legacy is the concept of the *Gesamtkunstwerk*: a synthesis of disparate art forms – dance and movement, light, design, music – into a total work of art. Wilson's major work, from *Deafman Glance* (1971) to the monumental but ill-fated *CIVIL warS* fifteen years later, may be seen as an attempt to realise a

Gesamtkunstwerk of and for our times. For Wilson's eclectic modernist sensibility is very much the fruit of the late-twentieth-century culture of televisual communication and image saturation. Unlike Craig's imagined artist of the future, he does not work merely with action, scene and voice, but also with playback, freeze-frame, slow motion and other related possibilities of video optics, such as superimposition and reverse negative.

Robert Wilson was born in Waco, Texas, in 1944. In the late fifties, he started a degree in business administration at the University of Texas, but he soon moved to the Pratt Institute, New York, to study painting and architecture; in 1965 he graduated with a Bachelor of Fine Arts degree. As a student, he quickly became involved in New York dance, theatre and film circles. At high school, he had entered a drama competition with an entirely non-verbal piece: 'Two people in white sat in a room. Now and then there would be a knock on the door. One of them would get up and open it, but there was nobody there. That was all. It became a key piece; I keep going back to it' (*The Observer*, 4 June 1978). In 1963 he created the celebrated giant puppet protagonists of 'Motel', the third part of Jean-Claude van Itallie's *America Hurrah!* In Texas, he had also undertaken some theatre projects with children. As a voluntary worker with the welfare department in New York, he extended this area of interest to encompass brain-damaged or hyperactive children and 'terminally handicapped' adults. Through simple physical exercises, Wilson explored the relationship between mental and physical activity. He soon came to believe that the release of psycho-physical tensions and the location of internal kinetic energies and expressive outlets in motor creativity could stimulate a mental responsiveness. As a child, Wilson himself had suffered from a severe speech impediment until at the age of seventeen he met Mrs Byrd Hoffman, a dancer in her seventies, who helped him release certain blocks and tensions through relaxation and movement; the impediment disappeared. He continued to hold teaching posts in various institutions in and around New York into the early seventies: animating children's theatre, often with difficult children considered 'subnormal', leading dance and psychosomatic movement therapy sessions with adults. There were performances of pieces by paraplegics, even a 'ballet' for bed-bound iron-lung patients. Indeed, participants in his workshops – 'ordinary people, borderline psychotics', according to one of them, Stefan Brecht – made up the kernel of performers involved in his early theatre work. Plays were born from the workshops, these idiosyncratic individuals clearly defined and located as such within Wilson's own highly structured settings. Wilson's main concern here was therapeutic: the facilitation of self-expression by refusing to accept that individual peculiarities or handicaps were deviations demanding to be erased. Instead, these idiosyncrasies were felt to be symptomatic of different modes of perception and being, inherently valuable both to the individual concerned and to the teacher. Difference was to be prized, stimulated and encouraged, not suppressed in a fallacious process of 'normalisation'.

The mid sixties saw Wilson pursuing a variety of concerns before concentrating his energies almost entirely on the creation of theatre pieces. Having worked with the futuristic architect Paolo Soleri in Arizona during the summer of 1966, in 1967 he was commissioned to create an enormous open-air sculptural environment, 'Poles', a mysterious arrangement of about 600 telegraph poles of differing lengths in a wheatfield in Ohio. Also in 1967, he collaborated at Jerome Robbins' American Theatre

Robert Wilson

Laboratory in New York, where he was able to watch the formalist choreographer Balanchine at work. After two minimalist public pieces – *Baby* (1967) and *Byrdwoman* (1968) with Meredith Monk – Wilson began work on his first major theatre work, *The King of Spain* (1969). The production coincided with the formal establishment of a group of collaborators, collectively the Byrd Hoffman School of Byrds, under the organisational umbrella of the non-profit making, tax-exempt Byrd Hoffman Foundation, a small body set up to administer Wilson's work; the unit still survives intact.

Staged in the vast and semi-derelict Anderson Theatre, *The King of Spain* contained in embryonic form the basic constituents that would characterise Wilson's work with the Byrds until *Einstein on the Beach* (1976). At this early stage, he manifested evidence of an innocent, even naïve, theatrical sensibility. All the illusion-making elements of theatre were brought to the fore and fully exploited: stage machinery (drops, traps, pulleys, and so on), elaborate painted backdrops, intricate lighting designs, the framed distancing of a 'stage picture' resultant from an imperative use of the proscenium arch. Wilson has always searched for a classical theatre of surface pretence. To this day, the stage remains for him a prestidigitator's box of tricks, an enchanted locus to be charged with surprises, wistful dreams and dark irrational imaginings. In *The King of Spain*, the four legs of a giant cat traversed the stage, its invisible body out of sight, imagined in the flies above the actors. Concealed microphones distorted and magnified tiny and otherwise inaudible stage sounds – chairs creaking, the pouring of liquids – or disoriented the audience by locating the source of a voice in some distant corner far from its apparent origins. In this way, peculiar but otherwise imperceptible vocal mannerisms and

227

textures could be conveyed in a heightened form to the detriment of the usual semantic significance of words. Wilson wanted to liberate the musical sound, colour and structure of language, as well as the individual's physical response to language chanted, intoned, ruptured or flatly declaimed.

Wilson's characteristic compositional approach was elaborated for the first time here. He selected a number of charged images, the fruit of his own or others' dreams and imaginings: the outsized cat's legs (reminiscent of Ionesco's *Amédée*); a fearsome King of Spain in an animal-like mask, seated with his back to the spectators in a high-backed chair; a Victorian drawing-room setting, its back wall shattered to reveal suggestions of a gentle Mediterranean countryside bathed in sunshine beyond. These were sketched, reworked, refined by Wilson in a frenzy throughout the rehearsal process, finally crystallising to determine the broad shape of a scene, its architectonic arrangement.[1] Within these formal givens, the inexperienced amateur performers would slowly and deliberately show themselves as they were, revealing the minutiae of habitual individual activities – incessant chattering, aimless wandering, fluttering hands, and a multitude of less obsessional tics – and widely different physical forms: Wilson's sparkling, regal eighty-eight-year-old grandmother; a pregnant woman; tiny children. One of the Byrds, an Ohio waitress called Susan Sheehy, stood 5 feet 5 inches and weighed 200 pounds (over 14 stone). Wilson's role as director–therapist was to liberate the individual natures and vocabularies of movement of the performers; to elaborate an unfixed score of sounds, movements and gestures sufficiently open structurally to permit the individual performers to act in accordance with their own profound individuality, without fracturing their awareness of their relationship to the group and to the space as a whole; to select and refine material and construct the spatial configurations within which to locate the activities; and finally to interweave the multifarious dynamics and textures to produce a kaleidoscopic theatre of images. In rehearsal, Wilson would give the performers purely physical choreographic directions, never psychological or interpretive instructions; he consistently refused to explain the 'meaning' of an image or a scene. He would firmly fix positions, entrances and exits, as well as the particular zone within which a movement or activity was to take place. Although specific cues would be set – normally at the beginning or end of another activity, although some were timed – he allowed the performer a great margin of freedom in terms of the length of an activity, the number of repetitions. So, from a lengthy period of collective movement therapy (with its echoes of Isadora Duncan, one of Wilson's few avowed influences) and vocal release work, Wilson draws impressions, fragments, moods, augmenting any traditional conception of a directorial role by confronting his personal responsibility as graphic artist, designer of settings and rigorously exacting lighting, choreographer, writer and eventually performer.

To a great extent, the nature of Wilson's theatre work was determined by chance encounters with two 'maladjusted' children, the first of whom was eleven-year-old Raymond Andrews, a deaf–mute black boy he met in New Jersey. Deafness (and later, with Christopher Knowles, what had been erroneously diagnosed as 'autism') offered Wilson evidence of alternative perceptual models, infinitely coherent and valid in themselves and perhaps superior to our 'normal' rational mode. Wilson felt that Andrews' paintings bore witness to an unfettered sensitivity to colour (which he appeared to be able to use to convey the nature of an individual object's or person's energy or activity) and to the dynamic relationships of figures to space. In addition, Andrews seemed to possess an extraordinary responsiveness to social situations, as well as to music and sound on a corporeal, vibratory level. He was, for Wilson, an 'accomplished artist' on a pre-rational level possessing a profound visual and kinaesthetic lucidity. Wilson believed that extensive contact with certain 'maladjusted' sensibilities and with the alternative channels of communication they exploited would promote in the other members of the group a liberation from socially imposed limitations (both physical and psychological) and a heightened awareness of different possibilities. The ultimate refinement of such work perhaps found its form – and fame – in Lucinda Childs' quirky obsessional dance of self-presentation in perpetual motion in *Einstein on the Beach*.

So Wilson and his group were attempting to adjust their own sensibilities, *not* to manipulate that of their models. Eventually they were able to learn to varying degrees alternative languages of communication and perceptual structures. By exploring and, increasingly, imitating Andrews' non-verbal body language and raw sounds in workshops, they developed a style of performance that was apparently anti-naturalistic in its broadest sense (non-narrative, non-verbal, psychologically acausal), yet for Wilson naturalistic in a profounder way. He suggests that everyone sees and hears on two different levels. In conscious cerebralisation, the stimuli of the external physical world are received by an 'exterior screen', the basis for assimilating most everyday impressions and information. There is, in addition, an 'interior screen' on which to see and hear; although one is only ever aware of it while dreaming, Wilson suggests, it is permanently in operation. The blind receive impressions largely on an interior visual screen, the deaf on an interior auditory screen, both of which have become infinitely more acutely developed than in 'normal' people. One of Wilson's primary aims in his early work was to create certain conditions which would induce a state of mind in the spectators in which the differentiation between 'internal' and 'external' becomes blurred, eventually fusing into one unified, unseparated mode of heightened perception. Broadly three areas of concern were explored to establish these conditions: the manipulation of time, the construction of visionary images, and the fracturing of verbal language.

Wilson reacted instinctively against the compression and condensation of time into the conventional theatrical time of the stage. He felt that the speed and surfeit of experience crammed into every moment was blinding to perception and communication. Instead he proposed an infinitesimal fragmentation and hallucinatory expansion of time to create a hypnotic, contemplative reality outside normal time, a reality in which time could be investigated as a spatial dimension. *Deafman Glance* (Nancy Festival, France, in 1971) with *The Life and Times of Sigmund Freud* tacked on as a fourth act, lasted for eight and a half hours. *Overture* (Paris, 1972), at twelve hours in length, was dwarfed by *KA MOUNTAIN AND GUARDenia TERRACE ('A story about a Family and Some People Changing')* at the Shiraz Festival, Iran, in the same year, which went on for seven days and nights. *The CIVIL warS*, planned for 1984 but never realised fully, was variously estimated to last for anything between nine and seventeen hours. For *The Life and Times of Joseph Stalin* (Brooklyn Academy of Music, 1973), seven acts in twelve hours, the spectators were invited to doze, sleep, go out to the lobby for refreshments as necessary or desirable. With the images as infinitely slowly evolving objects in themselves, time was established as peculiar to each activity within the image as a whole. Different rhythms and dynamics were deliberately set up in counterpoint. Sheryl Sutton's darkly ominous Byrdwoman figure, raven perched on one hand, remained totally immobile for inordinate periods – a charged inactivity which must also have had repercussions for the perceptual frame of mind of the performer, like Zazen meditation or the intricate abstract geometrics of the Noh theatre; every so often a runner traversed the stage behind Sutton at high speed, as if he had completed another circuit of some enormous imaginary course located far in the beyond; figures with fish tied to their backs crawled along the front edge of the stage laboriously. At one point, a tightrope walker crossed high above the space, only the legs visible; at other times and other speeds, a naked man, a roller-skater, a St Bernard dog and a lumbering mechanical turtle individually passed across the stage.

In itself, each activity constitutes a permanent present; yet in layered montage it is somehow located outside the exigencies of external time. Indeed, any sense of 'normal' time trickling past comes to feel unreal. One loses an awareness of time as being linear and sequential. In Wilson's world it is relative, pulsing in slow waves between focused points of tension and areas of 'selective inattention'. Never able to formulate a fixed whole, but with ample room to breathe imaginatively, the spectator is free and responsible to choose where he is in relation to the whole or a particular element within the whole: where to look, what to see. In Wilson's theatre, the spectator literally has time to enter fully, withdraw from and re-enter the flow of images at will, his free associative imaginings

encouraged to wander; liberated from any coercion to
attend intellectually, therein lies his participation. After a
lengthy period submerged in this decelerated reality, a
state of reduced consciousness may take him beyond
cerebral response, beyond boredom to a twilight state –
like Molly Bloom's half-sleeping, half-waking – a point of
renewal of certain perceptions, even hallucination of
elements not presented on-stage at all.[2]

Wilson's anti-intellectual aesthetic is built around
furnishing the spectator with an implacably beautiful flow
of images, in the widest sense of the word: temporal and
spatial configurations of sound, movement and their
relationship to space – above all, an architectonic
arrangement of simultaneously superimposed elements,
like overlaid slides, the contents of which are above all their
form. Intuitively constructed and ordered according to
lyrical, musical criteria, the various images are presented as
part of a continuously evolving tapestry, an apparently
self-generating pictorial series. (Wilson's favourite
metaphors are of watching clouds drift past, or gazing from
a train window while daydreaming.) The series is
nevertheless discontinuous in terms of the affect content of
individual images. His aesthetic shows no respect for
harmony and classical resolution, being coloured rather by
deliberately constructed dissonance, rupture and
dissociation at all levels: between gesture and
verbalisation, between activity and setting, between
textures, moods, dynamics, habitual frames of reference.
The images have the quality of 'visions', fascinating
associational ideograms which 'emanate' unaccountably
(and therein lies one of the substantial points of contact
with the surrealist images of Dali, Duchamp, de Chirico
and above all Magritte). In constant mobility, their
ideational content remains always out of reach,

indeterminate, evasive and non-representational, for they make no reference to a specific external reality; constantly moving in and out of focus as they gradually evolve, they are irreducible objects encouraging the constant mobilisation of a vast network of momentary evocations.

Denied any of the structural supports traditionally employed to guide his responses, the spectator is lulled into a contemplation of the stage space as an encompassing reality within which the dynamics of evolution, change and transformation are precisely what he becomes aware of. The images are structured in juxtaposition, as in dreams (or *Alice in Wonderland*), with scant deference to the logic of linear narrative development or the laws of physics; chairs fly into and out of the space, an eye lights up in the tip of a pyramid (the masonic sign on a dollar note) before the tip in its entirety lifts off and disappears into the flies. These images are Wilson's most crystalline challenge to the limitations of the 'imprisoning' rationality of perception on 'external screens' alone. They offer a procession of moving pictures across the energy field of a stage, culled from the remotest corners of human consciousness, the dumping ground for private neuroses as well as half-remembered fragments of popular mythology and hagiography. The performance is the projection of a film of a mental landscape in which the configurations are Wilson's own, marked by a perfectionist's eye for detail, a painter's formal compositional and tonal sensitivity – from the monochromatic severity of *Patio* (1977) and *Death, Destruction and Detroit* (1979) to the Disneyland technicolour of certain sections of *Stalin* – and an architect's intuitive feel for the dynamics and tensions of spatial relationships. And yet, paradoxically, although the film remains within Wilson's own mental landscape, its coherence for the spectator does not result from his sensing the omnipresence of one ordering subjective intelligence or creative awareness. These reflections of deep mental processes take on a starkly impersonal archetypal quality, an 'objective' reality.

In June 1971, *Les Lettres françaises* published an open letter written by Louis Aragon as if to André Breton, who had died fifteen years earlier. As one of the founding protagonists of the original surrealist movement almost half a century earlier, Aragon described the revelation that Wilson's *Deafman Glance* offered him. Particularising the piece as an 'extraordinary freedom machine', and its eighty-seven performers as 'experimenters in a science still nameless, that of the body and its freedom,' he suggested it heralded 'the wedding of gesture and silence, of movement and the ineffable'. He went on to proclaim that this silent

34. *Deafman Glance* (1971): Raymond Andrews, silently observing the images unfolding beneath him; behind him, the pyramid

somnolent reverie, an 'opera for the deaf' created around a deaf boy (Raymond Andrews) was the miracle the surrealists had awaited:

> I never saw anything more beautiful in the world since I was born. Never has any play come anywhere near this one, because it is at once life awake and the life of closed eyes, the confusion between everyday life and the life of each night; reality mingles with dream, all that's inexplicable in the life of a deaf man. . . . It is what we others, we who fathered surrealism . . . dreamt it might become after us, beyond us. . . .[3]

It is pertinent indeed to see Wilson as an artist in a direct line of descent from surrealism, a legacy immediately apparent in his emphasis on the subliminal power of delirious 'convulsive images', on a pre-rational poetry of incongruity, savage beauty and acausal dreamscapes. In addition, Wilson's relationship to language and text smacks of surrealist automatic writing and dadaist collage, the determination that their creators shared with Artaud to 'shatter language' in order to touch life itself.

Wilson's written texts are made up of a discontinuous montage of fragments from diverse sources. For example, *A Letter for Queen Victoria* and *Patio* both include deliberately half-heard snatches of dialogue from old 'B' movies and American *film noir*. By leaving the television on for long periods (or more than one television simultaneously), Wilson assimilates a flood of verbal splinters in an area of unconscious peripheral hearing while engaged in some other activity, such as painting; much later, he writes down a slightly distorted, deformed version in the manner of Burroughs. Similarly, *$ Value of Man* was built almost entirely around insidiously repetitive TV advertisements as reshaped perceptually by the mind of an 'autistic' child, Christopher Knowles (see below). In *Stalin*, some of the material was drawn directly from discussions of problems in rehearsal: 'Keep that line!', 'But what does it mean?'

Wilson's early works were remarkable for their Beckettian use of silence as a charged entity and for the deliberate inconsistency of vocal projection. Often no attempt was made to communicate to the auditorium what was said on-stage, the spectator merely picking up traces of inaudible mumblings and mutterings. Like much of Gertrude Stein's writing, Hugo Ball's dadaist poems or Robert Desnos' surrealist trances, Wilson's texts are often structured musically as tone poems: obsessively repetitive, an associational aural collage possessing a shamanic incantatory quality. The performers seem to be possessed, oracular ciphers of some indecipherable but authentic experience. The interactional exchange of dialogue is never established; instead it is disrupted or parodied.

Discursive meaning itself is usually undercut through the juxtaposition and simultaneous counterpoint of voices, whether united in a recitative chorale, isolated in parodies of rhetoric or set against pre-recorded music in a sort of vocal Varèse. At moments the text swoops towards a nodal point of apparently cogent rational ideation, before beating a hasty retreat into irrational non-sequiturs, burblings, screams, or the meaningless paralinguistic debris of everyday conversation: 'huh', 'what', 'Hmm', 'yup', 'OK', 'well', or invented sounds such as 'spups', 'birrup'. The text of *Patio*, for example, seems to contain a fumbling attempt at a description of what it is we are witnessing – 'all things are subject to accidentally qualities in a big static space that forms the sculpture' – before departing into an entirely new area, seemingly unconnected: 'catch me later maybe I will'; 'what kind of child was he . . .'.

The performers somehow suggest being lured unwillingly by some compulsive force demanding verbalisation. Their simultaneous counter-resistance seems to come as the direct result of the inability of words to meet the more extreme moments of consciousness and imagination. The dynamic tension between these two contrary impulses serves to fragment and distort the word further, as well as providing a characteristic undercurrent of uncomfortable malaise. As for Artaud, Brook, Grotowski and the surrealistis in their own linguistic experiments, Wilson's interest is to uncover a music of new sounds and shapes, sliding forms compounded in a process of wilful disintegration. Is it possible to burst through the confines of denotative fixed forms, to scrabble through a verbal scree of broken phonemes towards a vital and evolving 'essence', a radiant but inarticulate energy which communicates at a pre-cognitive, subliminal level?

Much of the stimulus for this reappraisal of the nature and role of verbal language came from Wilson's work with Christopher Knowles, a boy seriously brain-damaged from birth. The obsessive behavioural patterns of this 'autistic' child were seen by Wilson as evidence of imaginatively coherent daydreaming on a highly developed 'interior screen'. Wilson first came into contact with Knowles when he was sent a tape the boy had made. Playing with a cassette recorder, he had stopped, started, overdubbed to produce a fractured layering of rhythms and sounds. Wilson saw in Knowles' different mode of perception a similarity with his own concerns; he therefore learnt how to communicate with and encourage Knowles, locating outlets for his creativity. Knowles' tapes and writings subsequently formed the basis of *$ Value of Man* and *A Letter for Q. V.*

(the first performance for which a text was published); earlier they were included in *Stalin*, two particularly memorable highlights being a poem entitled 'Emily Likes the TV' and another, 'The Sundance Kid' (in Act I, scene iv), from which this short extract is taken:

The sundance kid was beautiful
The sundance kid was very very very beautiful
To know the sundance kid dances a lot
The sundance kid was beautiful
The sundance kid was very very very very beautiful
Up in the air
The sundance kid was beautiful
Yeah boom
Yeah the sundance kid was beautiful
Yeah the sundance kid was light brown brown
A kind of yellow
Something like that
Brown a kind of yellow

Knowles went on to collaborate with Wilson on a number of smaller-scale pieces: *DIA LOG/A MAD MAN A MAD GIANT A MAD DOG A MAD FACE A MAD URGE* (1974), *DIA LOG* (1975–6), *DIA LOG/NETWORK* (1978), *DIA LOG/CURIOUS GEORGE* (1979–80).

All of Wilson's early work until 1973 was really one single developing piece, involving amateur 'Byrd' performers. (After 1973, the number of Byrds involved gradually diminished, until they were replaced entirely by professional performers). *Stalin* contained sections of all the previous performances: the whole of *The King of Spain* and *The Life and Times of Sigmund Freud*, most of *Deafman Glance* and fragments of both *Overture* and *KA*

MOUNTAIN. The last act was made up of new material. The production was epic in every sense: twelve hours in length, with 144 performers, including the dance critic Edwin Denby, Stefan Brecht, five children from the New York School for the Deaf and a seven-month-old baby, as well as a bestiary of assorted animals (a live goat, dog, sheep and boa constrictor, and a number of fake animals: a walrus, a turtle, polar and grizzly bears, ostriches, a camel,

35. *The Life and Times of Joseph Stalin* (1973): The Ostrich dance

a pink elephant), which served to tip the whole further towards magic and mystery. Protagonists included Queen Victoria, several Stalins, Sigmund and Anna Freud (the former performed by someone Wilson happened to see one day walking through Grand Central Station), Wilhelm Reich, King Philip of Spain, Helen Keller, Alexander

Graham Bell, Ivan the Terrible and Icarus. The production used 18,000 pounds of scenery, comprising twenty-one major sets, which were financed by the Gulbenkian Foundation.

Freud, Queen Victoria, Stalin, and subsequently Einstein and Hess (the unnamed central figure of *Death, Destruction and Detroit*) – what is the role of such figures within Wilson's work? Although a wealth of biographical material is fed into the performances piecemeal, they are never really *about* any of these figures. In the *New York Times* (14 Dec 1973), Wilson referred to *Stalin* as 'a time construction of the 20th century' as seen through 'one of its forces'. These figures act merely as starting points for a metaphorical examination of or meditation upon the central human concerns and myths of our time; the performances are above all a 'progression of spaces' associatively structured around a central figure. Wilson has said that, instead of Stalin, he might just as well have chosen Chaplin or Hitler. In Brazil in 1974, *Stalin* was performed as *The Life and Times of Dave Clark* in deference to a politically sensitive climate; Wilson was quite happy to use the name of a little-known Canadian criminal he had read about.

Wilson's next major work, the celebrated *Einstein on the Beach*, was first shown at the Avignon Festival in July 1976. This five-hour opera, the most elaborate and expensive spectacle to date (it cost almost US $1 million to stage), subsequently had its American première in November 1976 at the Metropolitan Opera, New York, the Everest of formal American culture. It marked Wilson's first extensive collaboration with professional performers, including the dancer Lucinda Childs, one of the original founders of the Judson Church Dance Theatre in the early sixties, and his first commissioning of a full score by a composer, Philip Glass. Wilson's libretto included texts by Christopher Knowles and a mass of semi-biographical details from the life of Einstein, researched extensively by both Wilson and Glass; in particular they latched onto his Romantic mysticism, his reputation as an innocent dreamer, his love of music. The usual stream of visual and aural oneiric images, entirely freed from the constraints of conventional dramatic narrative, was structured mathematically. Each of the four acts was preceded and followed by a 'knee-play', intermezzi which taken together formed a coherent piece in themselves. Each act was divided into three scenes, a dominant visual image recurring every third scene: a train–building; a courtroom and a bed; a field with a spaceship.

Philip Glass's music was written during the preparatory process in response to Wilson's evolving architectonic sketches, ultimately the basis for the set designs. As a series of hypnotic tonal colours patterned through augmentation, diminution and juxtaposition like oriental music, the score offered a perfect complement to and reflection of Wilson's concerns. The recurrence of visual motifs was echoed in the music's cyclical additive structure, its exploration of the interrelationship of stasis and movement. Through the repetition of minutely developing phrases and simple harmonic progressions, and a chanted chorale of numbers and the sol-fa syllables (do, re, mi, etc.), the structure became immediately audible, the process perceptible. The music's machine-like form was its dominant content, its libretto – uniquely made up of these primary elements of tonal and rhythmic structuring – descriptive only of itself.

Once again Wilson wove a tapestry of gestural, auditory and imaginal leitmotifs. Given the temporal concern at the heart of Einstein's research, and having discovered that the young scientist had worked in a patent office dealing

Robert Wilson

primarily with clocks while he was elaborating his theory of relativity, Wilson made frequent use in performance of a variety of instruments for the measurement of time. One clock went back an hour every twenty minutes, another had its face covered by a black disc with two small lights set into it – an allusion to the eclipse of 1919 that proved Einstein's theory of the curvature of space. A gyroscope moved ever further along a wire suspended above the stage, representing the passage of time. Wilson also insisted upon the obsessive repetition of certain geometrical angles and shapes, particularly triangles; apparently representing the fixity of a Euclidean conception of the universe, these forms contrasted with Einstein's revolutionary vision of a space–time continuum (evoked in the music and plastic images). Most of the performers were dressed in an

36.   *Einstein on the Beach* (1976): Left to right: Lucinda Childs, Dana Reitz and Sheryl Sutton; in the background, a slowly moving train

Einstein 'uniform' – plain white shirt, baggy trousers and braces. A solitary violinist, made up to resemble the familiar image of the mature Einstein (tousle-haired, with luxuriantly drooping moustache, and so on), looks on from a position of detachment near the orchestra pit; is this 'trial of science' his dream? Thematically the piece seemed to be concerned with a loss of innocence concomitant on technological advancement, the abuses of scientific knowledge, the attendant dehumanisation of ordinary people, the imminence of an apocalypse; the title's allusion to Nevil Shute's novel *On the beach* is no accident. Ultimately, significance is ambiguous, inconclusive. For the penultimate scene, a spectacular vision of the future in a nuclear age, we were taken inside a spaceship which had been seen approaching, on a wire, during the course of the performance. It was a complex of cellular modules, flashing lights and throbbing synthetic pulses. In the final scene, two solitary figures confronted each other in a featureless, post-Armageddon 'no man's land'; they appeared to be lovers on a moonlit beach.

In 1977, Wilson changed direction (partly to offset substantial debts after *Einstein*) to stage a chamber piece of altogether more modest and austere proportions, despite its cumbersome title: *I was sitting on my patio this guy appeared I thought I was hallucinating* (also known as *Patio*). The full title comes from the opening lines of a forty-five-minute monologue Wilson had written, a montage assemblage of fragments of *film noir* stories. Most were of tension and failure, but were underscored by a sombre humour; all remained unresolved. Suggestions abounded of suppressed violence, an unspecified anguish, even of imminent nervous breakdown. However, the fragments refused to coalesce into any overt narrative significance; the piece remained a tone poem of sinister elegance and languid menace. For the first act, Wilson directed himself performing the text; Lucinda Childs delivered a contrasting version of the same text in Act II. As Vivian Mercier once said of *Waiting for Godot*, 'nothing happens, twice'.

The performance as a whole was as minimalist and monochromatic as the 'living sculptures' of Gilbert and George, as claustrophobic as a monodrama. Once again, the basic image was constructed according to formal, architectural criteria of harmony and proportion: a black and white interior with three tall narrow windows set into a black back wall. During a prologue, the windows were open, a bright diffused light beyond a uniformly white drop casting long diagonal shafts and shadows into the space, which pulsed with energy and tension.[4] The performers, both clothed in black and white, were silhouetted. For the central section of each act, the windows filled with bookshelves, the space darkened, focused, closed in upon itself. For an epilogue, during which the last few lines are repeated, back wall and bookcases disappeared; the room was filled anew with a liberating light. The only objects within this rectilinear reductivist decor possessed fine clear sculptural lines, uncompromisingly modernist and 'unhomely', as well as possessing particular relationships to light; surfaces reflected, absorbed or distorted light. The objects were a steel couch, a champagne glass on a glass shelf, a brushed aluminium and glass table, a glass of water and a telephone. A small screen down-stage right relayed film images simultaneous with the 'action'; images included a ringing telephone, the actual 'phone now left off the hook. Body microphones provided a further dislocatory effect, the disembodied text becoming a stream-of-consciousness voice-over, the disjointed utterances of a mind wandering freely. Both acts were accompanied by a score composed by Alan Lloyd (piano for Act I, clavichord for Act II). Wilson's performance was steeped in scarcely suppressed hysteria; he suggested a fraught, self-defeating Fred Astaire. The second act was a quite different experience. Childs' tensions remained more discreet and equivocal, her hysteria more internalised, her minimal spiral movements more closely related to a recognisable conception of choreography; Lauren Bacall or Bette Davis sprang to mind.

By this time, Wilson had become a virtual expatriate. As the 'darling' of art-theatre circles in Europe, his work was lauded and championed; however, he has remained a peripheral figure in the United States, where financial aid has often been unforthcoming owing to the prohibitive expense of staging many of his productions. His next two major productions, both in 1979, were commissioned and produced in Europe: *Death, Destruction and Detroit* (at the Schaubühne am Halleschen Ufer, Berlin, in February) and *Edison* (at the Théâtre de Paris, Paris, in October). For *Death, Destruction and Detroit (DDD)*, Wilson returned to the epic proportions of his earlier work. The result was five-and-a-quarter-hour 'opera' in two acts (ironically referred to in the text as 'A Love Story in 16 Scenes'). Wilson considers it his best work to date, the most successful in terms of text and visual imagery; it has continued to fascinate him into the 1980s.

This period marks the apogee of Wilson's experiments, his veneration and celebration of light as an active dynamic protagonist, a vibrant spatial determinant as flexible and evocative as music. In a review of *Edison* in the *New York Times* (30 Oct 1979), John Rockwell described Wilson as a 'mystic of light'. There is a clear debt to the writings and designs of the Swiss visionary theoretician Adolphe Appia, forefather of modern theatre lighting. In his seminal work

Music and Production (*Die Musik und die Inscenierung*, 1899), Appia had detailed suggestions for the staging of Wagner in terms of rhythmic space, formal shape, colour and, above all, light. He had dreamed of a neo-Platonic theatre of intimation and suggestion within which light would be the primary agent for the implication and activation of the numinosity of space, the brush with which to paint the vision. For the mixed group of performers involved in *DDD* – young unknown professionals, a number of old cabaret artists, a company of amateurs of diverse age, plus four of Stein's Schaubühne company (including Otto Sander and Sabine Andreas) – there were five months of preparation, including an unprecedented three and a half weeks devoted exclusively to full-costume lighting rehearsals. The final performance manifested Wilson's sensitivity to the affective and spatial possibilities of light and shadows. In a number of minutely detailed chiaroscuro images, Wilson established himself as the modern theatre's Caravaggio in his treatment of statuesque and often immobile figures set against his own backdrops. In themselves, these drops created extraordinary moments of ominous tension, focus and mobility within immobility. Their characteristically broad diagonal lacerations possessed the velocity, rhythms and dark spatial energies of the frantic graphite and ink sketches that were their source; these were blown up photographically and reworked through re-exposure and realignment before being painted onto the drops using the conventional grid method. In terms of lighting-effects, for scene 9 Wilson borrowed as backdrop Albert Speer's original design for a Nuremberg rally: eighty spots located in the floor at the back of the space projected parallel beams vertically, to create a veritable wall of light. The cost of this one effect contributed to the abandonment of a projected revival of

Directors' Theatre

37. *Death, Destruction and Detroit* (1979): Wilson's own
backdrop: mobility within immobility

DDD at the Metropolitan Opera, New York, in summer
1979.

The starting point and central figure of *DDD* was the
former Nazi deputy Rudolf Hess, although Wilson kept
this a secret from the German press and audiences; indeed,
a photograph of Hess was deleted from the programme at
the request of the Schaubühne producers, who felt it to be
misleading and too sensitive politically. As a result Hess's
presence within the piece went largely unnoticed at the
time, although foreknowledge of it would have made a
significant difference to the spectator's perception of the
work as a whole. As usual, a famous figure was treated as a
numinous focal point for a formal investigation of what
radiates from it within the playground of Wilson's own
imagination. Given Wilson's poetic, conceptual concerns,
the figure in question inevitably becomes both
depoliticised and aestheticised; perhaps justifiably, Wilson

248

has been attacked by the broad left throughout his career
for his apolitical, even reactionary, formalism. Wilson
found his initial stimulus in a photographic image of Hess
raking leaves within the Spandau compound; this one
image became the occasion for another epic Wilsonian
associational daydream. Wilson was startled by certain
formal elements of the photo – the quality of light on Hess's
hand and stick, his withdrawn blank expression
foreshortened by a degree of over-exposure, the texture of
the prison wall. He made a huge number of copies which he
enlarged to the point of dissolution of significance, echoing
the way in which human activity had been treated in the
early works; all that remained were compositional
abstractions of greys and whites.

He then commenced research into the figure of Hess,
uncovering a 'mysterious madman', a 'footnote to Hitler'
who lives on in the solitude of a 'prison-palace'. In final
performance, a mass of allusions were made to certain
biographical details, some familiar (the Nuremberg rallies;
Hess's abortive solo flight and parachute landing in
Scotland; Spandau prison), others more obscure to us. One
scene enacted a notorious incident when the young Hess
placed a handful of earth from the four corners of Germany
beneath his baby son's cradle. In performance, this
fragment was portrayed without introduction or exegesis as
a painfully slow ceremony, gradually developing into a tap
dance and eventually a bizarre ritualistic series of wild
movements, atavistic and fanatical. In another scene, in
Hess's prison cell, Spandau's solitary prisoner was a
self-absorbed old man dancing in silence to a Keith Jarrett
piano improvisation. As the space filled with waltzing
couples in full evening dress, he continued unabashed,
ignoring them until they finally faded away into dark
corners; once again, he was an old man dancing alone. Frau

Ilse Hess and Hitler's architect Albert Speer – the latter originally imprisoned in Spandau with Hess – also appeared within the piece; Hitler, Goering and Dresden were referred to in the text, and there were echoes of monumentally cumbersome Nazi architecture in the designs (for instance in scene 7, 'A Contemporary Interior'). Above all, suggestions of Frau Hess's devotion and compassion recurred. The play's final image showed an old woman quietly lamenting her solitude, confronted by a huge, featureless and impenetrable wall. The form of the performance had been poignantly circular, for it had begun with the lone figure of Hess on the *other* side of the same wall. The subtitle referred us to Frau Hess's 'love story'.

It is possible to trace loosely some of the strands of the performance's associative development, a chain of collective clichés from popular mythology led through a maze of spatial and temporal leaps and incongruities by Wilson's private imaginings. So, for example, in scene 3 the figure of a parachutist (Hess) hung suspended above a group of berobed judges or priests; in a scene charged with a sense of chastisement and retribution, they danced, gesticulating at the impotent sacrificial figure above with their neon sticks.[5] From Hess's fascination with flying (evinced by his journals) and the above allusion to his most famous journey by 'plane, Wilson contrived to imagine a meditation by Hess in Spandau on the future space race. This led to a number of science-fiction scenes; the programme located scene 4 'in the future, a thousand years later, on a different planet during an electrical storm', and scene 16 involved a race between two ovoid cars 'somewhere in a future desert'. Man's future technological capabilities were juxtaposed with scenes of his terrestrial origins and ancestors; spectators witnessed, for example, the battles of prehistoric creatures, including two psychedelic dinosaurs, 'one big and green, the other, small, fat and red'. The conquest of space was further linked both to Nazi *Lebensraum* (expansionism) and to the myths of the Wild West; in scene 10, depicting what the programme called 'a mythical struggle close to our time', cowboys and Indians battled in a Western landscape.

The text was constructed in English entirely by Wilson. For the performance, it was translated by the Schaubühne *Dramaturg* Peter Krumme into German, a language of which Wilson has almost no knowledge. In rehearsal, his only textual suggestions to the actors related to rhythmic and tonal form. His concern was to arrange the material architecturally, spatially, as an integral component in the artificial construction of image configurations. In performance, the text was apprehended by the spectator as a musical structure, a score of recurrent rhythmic and tonal

38. *Death, Destruction and Detroit*: The impermanence and fragility of relationships, set against a Wilson trompe l'oeil drop

motifs. As in *Patio*, the primary semantic suggestion was of the impermanence of relationships; scenically and textually, the audience was offered fragments of fleeting encounters, departures, absences, unfulfilled desires, the loneliness of separation, memory, the passage of time. As the performance developed, semantic frameworks and apparent structures of exchange were increasingly ruptured. The incidence of echo and repetition heightened until a breaking-point was reached, when verbalisation collapsed into a juxtaposition of separate voices, or the separate constituent elements of the original whole.

The power of the production lay in its images. For example, in the scene entitled 'The Kitchen', a mother in a long black dress read a fairytale about Mother Bear and Red Robin to a small child on a tiny chair. They were inside an empty white room, at the centre of which hung a surreal oversized lightbulb. The child, a book in his lap, listened attentively while eating a green apple. The atmosphere of gently domestic suppression and confinement finally shattered at the end of the scene with the appearance of an elephant's trunk. The child quietly climbed into it; liberated, he floated away out of sight and into another reality. This image reflected the enchantment Wilson hopes to elicit from the acquiescent spectator, open to his magical reveries. Like the elephant's trunk, they exist above all as temporary 'freedom machines', inviting access to an exploration of and revelatory confrontation with the poetic sources of our own imaginations, their fears, hopes and dreams.

In the early eighties, Wilson continued to provoke acclaim and outrage in equal measures, with a small number of beautiful, if short-lived, works. The most notable of these was *Great Day in the Morning* (1981), a piece built around the dignity and hope inherent in the sources of black spirituals, and produced by Wilson in collaboration with his friend the opera singer Jessye Norman. Recently Wilson was awarded the Pulitzer Prize by the advisory panel, only to be rejected by the Pulitzer Board, a situation echoing that of Hemingway in 1940 with *For Whom the Bell Tolls*. The monumental *CIVIL warS* project, envisaged by Wilson as an intercultural 'shooting star', fell victim to the indifference of American funding bodies. Ironically, the work that would have brought Wilson's imagination back to an American audience stumbled at the last financial hurdle; despite massive financial commitment from those countries around the world involved in the production – Japan, France, Italy, Germany, Holland – last-minute support from the Los Angeles Olympic Arts Committee was unforthcoming. The project, whose separate parts had already been performed in their countries of origin, contained a pageant

39.   *CIVIL warS* (1984): The Rotterdam section

40.   *CIVIL warS*: The Cologne section

of mythical and historical figures, including Voltaire, Frederick the Great, Mata Hari, General Lee, the photographer Matthew Brady, Henry IV, Karl Marx, Don Quixote, Admiral Perry, various characters from the works of Jules Verne, Marie Curie, Abraham Lincoln and his wife, Joan of Arc, Garibaldi, Hercules, Hopi Indians, ninjas, dancing and singing giraffes, lions, tigers, zebras and giant traveller parrots. After last-gasp attempts to salvage the project, including a proposed simultaneous broadcast of the projects from around the world, had come to nothing, Wilson was left embittered and heavily in debt.

There is one positive element to have emerged from the sorry *CIVIL warS* saga. It marked the genesis of a continuing friendship and collaboration between Wilson and a writer of considerable weight and maturity, the East German Heiner Müller, formerly *Dramaturg* with the Berliner Ensemble. Wilson and Müller first came together on the Cologne section of *CIVIL warS*, by all accounts the strongest; there, the friction of juxtaposing Müller's emotionally fraught, densely imagistic texts with the distanced formality of Wilson's staging produced surprising creative sparks, the one illuminating and feeding the other. In October 1984, Müller's *Medea* texts ('Despoiled Shore', 'Medeamaterial' and 'Landscape with Argonauts') served as prologue to Wilson's operatic version of Euripides' *Medea* (Lyons Opera and the Festival d'Automne, Paris) with music by the British minimalist Gavin Bryars. Finally, in 1986, two new works have brought Wilson back to American audiences, with fresh acclaim. Müller's *Hamletmachine* was staged by Wilson at New York University with an amateur student cast. The piece is a plotless but astringent meditation on Hamlet and Ophelia, sexual politics and the 1956 Hungarian uprising, studded with a myriad of other, more obscure political, psychological and historical allusions. In part 4 of Müller's text, Hamlet splits the heads of Marx, Lenin and Mao with an axe; in another scene, an actor tears in half a photograph of Müller himself with great deliberation and ceremony. Then in March 1986 came Wilson's first full confrontation with a classic text, which seems to have focused and not restricted his outlandish imagination; his first major première in the United States for a full decade, it was an unquestionable commercial success. His version of Euripides' *Alcestis*, with a prologue by Müller, was produced by Robert Brustein's American Repertory Theatre at Cambridge, Massachusetts. Having already been engaged to stage a version of Gluck's *Alceste* at the Stuttgart Opera at the end of 1986, Wilson was intrigued by the possibility of pairing the two very different works in the same year. (Similarly, Wilson's version of Euripides' *Medea* had been paired with a simultaneous production, also in Lyons, of the first revival for almost 300 years of Marc-Antoine Charpentier's baroque opera *Médée* [1693], with the original French libretto by Thomas Corneille.)

In his prologue, a thirteen-page unbroken sentence called 'Description of a Picture', Müller presents us with what he describes as 'a synthetic fragment of a landscape beyond death'.[6] He has publicly detailed his sources for the piece: a drawing in his possession, the Noh play *Kumanaka*, book XI of *The Odyssey*, and Alfred Hitchcock's *The Birds*. He has appropriated and redefined elements from these sources into an entirely new whole, a process Wilson saw fit to extend in production. Originally entitled 'Explosion of a Memory', in performance the prologue was delivered in a fragmented form on tape by overdubbed and intercut voices (including those of Christopher Knowles and Robert Brustein), overlapping with live voices on stage; largely desemanticised and almost entirely incoherent, the piece was treated musically, Wilson contriving to create a distance between sound and image. Müller's original text both echoes the death and rebirth themes in Euripides, and reflects a number of Wilson's major production images and themes: birds, rock falls, the mountain range, the three trees, an eye, the relationship between death and sex.

For the performance's central section, Wilson dismantled a translation of Euripides by Dudley Fitts and Robert Fitzgerald, rewriting and reassembling to create his own distinctive collage. Wilson's text is essentialised, stripped of psychology; the choral odes are almost entirely absent. In performance, certain key words were repeated as a refrain both on tape and live ('nothing', 'death'). Wilson also wove in excerpts from Rainer Maria Rilke's poem *Alkestis* and from Müller's prologue, his determining

256

criteria once again musical and affective. To underpin the performance as a whole, Hans-Peter Kühn designed an 'audio environment', a taped montage of sound-effects: dog barks, bird cries, the ticking of clocks, and at the very end what sounded like the roar of helicopters circling unseen above (in fact the amplified noise of a boiler underneath the rehearsal rooms in Cambridge). For the Cambridge première, this central section was followed by an anonymous Japanese Kyogen play, the seventeenth-century *Birdcatcher in Hell*: an oasis of riotous slapstick comedy parodying the lofty sacrifices and recriminations of Euripides, further enlivened by a Laurie Anderson score. All three sections of the performance were variations on a central theme, that of death and rebirth, their tone variously macabre and trivial, sublimely meditative and grotesquely knockabout.

The staging of *Alcestis* is pure Wilson. With classical symmetry, three cypress trees were transformed in turn into temple columns and finally (when Hercules, a fur-clad frontiersman, rescued Alcestis from Hades) three chimneystacks belching smoke, radiant fissures appearing in their sides. In this way epic temporal movement was suggested, from a natural pre-industrial state to contemporary nuclear technology (were the cracks images of a core meltdown?). From the representational, even nostalgic, to the abstract and contemporary, Wilson's eclecticism and cultural relativism reflect the identity crisis of post-modernism. Admetus's father struggled and wheezed, imprisoned within an oxygen bubble. Alcestis's death scene – with alarm clocks, a radio, a real modern bed, Admetus in pyjamas – contained apparent anachronisms, but these trappings of the contemporary bourgeoisie were depoliticised and rendered alien when located in the aural–visual environment, removed from a habitual frame of reference. Their 'otherness' was compounded by Wilson's own luxuriant lighting and by the abstract gestural choreography developed for the production by the Japanese classical dancer Suzushi Hanayagi, in which movement was rarely illustrative.

An invisible stream divided the front of the stage from the back. At the beginning and end of the performance, an unidentified young woman glided effortlessly along its course, her arms outstretched in some hieratic gesture of silent lament. Other women washed their hair and clothes in the stream. Like Ganga in Brook's *Mahabharata*, the stream carried a double charge: source of ritual ablution and renewal, and place of death, a Styx. Death, a huge white insect–birdman or harpy, rose up through the stone blocks of the back wall. This chorus-figure was represented by a 20-foot androgynous Cycladic statue, a smaller (human) figure harnessed to its abdomen, wrapped in mummy bandages. In the central section, apparently solid granite boulders rolled gently and silently down a mountainous scree as 'invisible spirits move[d] underground'. Embedded in the shards of rock were fragments of archaeological artefacts, silent testaments to the evanescence of cultural forms: the prow of a Viking ship, ancient Chinese terracotta funerary figures, a primitive carved stone head – pitted, worn, broken. References were recognisably multi-cultural, distant from the original Greek context. Perhaps this *Alcestis* could be seen as a tragedy of cultural impermanence, the collapse and death of civilisations and their forms, rather than the individual tragedy of the central psychological narrative, the story of Alcestis: the mountain debris as the scree of culture? At the end of the performance, a green laser beam projected an eye onto the mountain's flank, then gouged a hole in it; through this opening, a seeping wound, was suggested the presence of glowing magma just below the surface.

Wilson chose to eliminate Euripides' restorative 'happy ending', instead finding a positive force in the tale's ambiguous irresolution. Hercules re-emerged from Hades with the veiled figure of a woman, which then fragmented into three identical figures. The spectator could not be certain which of them, if any, was Alcestis. As these mysterious hooded women sat silent and immobile on rocks – Alcestis is forbidden to speak for three days on her return – the discomfort of her husband, King Admetus, grew. The audience were left to wonder what these figures would say and do at the end of their period of silence.

Wilson's current concerns revolve around finding the means to relaunch the *CIVIL warS* project. In the meantime he plans to pursue this new direction in his work with a production of another classic text; he has been commissioned to direct *King Lear* in Hamburg in September 1987, in a German translation by Heiner Müller. The story of Lear has intrigued Wilson for many years – one section of *KA MOUNTAIN* was drawn from Shakespeare's text, and it is surely no coincidence that the impact of losing a loved one was thematically at the very heart of both *Freud* and *Stalin*. He claims his interest now lies in the play's comic possibilities and its structural formalism. For the part of Lear, he has already engaged an old German comedian who spends most of his life in a mental institution. Before *Lear*, however, Wilson is to stage *Death, Destruction and Detroit Part 2*, again at the Schaubühne in Berlin, in February 1987. Just as Hess was the focal point for the first version, Franz Kafka will be at the heart of this new work, which is to be based on his letters and diaries.

In the course of his career, Wilson has taken the practice

of scenic writing to its logical conclusion. We have traced the origin of scenic writing in the political work of Brecht and we have seen how it was developed by Littlewood, Planchon, Stein and others. There is nothing overtly political about Wilson's theatre: it might appear to stand more in the tradition of Grotowski and Brook, with its interest in therapy and its concern to probe the most fundamental levels of human awareness, communication and interpersonal relationships. Moreover, his control over every aspect of each production recalls Craig's vision of the single presiding artistic imagination at work in the theatre of the future. However, it would be a mistake to make too much of this control and to see Wilson merely as the exploiter of his performers, as if he treated them as raw materials with no creative freedom of their own. On the contrary, he leaves them considerable freedom and relies on their creative input to fill out the images or scenes of his productions. It would be equally mistaken to categorise his work as pure formalism. Though often hermetic, and containing no easy slogans, his productions embody in their very shape and method comments on both philosophical and political values. They achieve this by a highly developed use of the alienating effects that were the hallmark of Brechtian theatre practice. In particular, Wilson exploits the technique of using each element on the stage to undercut, contradict or comment on the others. Unlike most directors, he is content for these separate expressive elements to remain fragmented. He resists the temptation to synthesis and in this he manifests his critical commentary on our fragmented age. His productions do not, as Brook's so often do, end on an evocation of harmony and resolution.

In his researches into non-verbal communication, he does however resemble both Brook and Grotowski; like them he is sometimes treated as a prophet and guru. He also resembles Planchon in his search for a theatre of vivid and complex images. He differs sharply from Littlewood, Mnouchkine and Stein in not having started out with an objective defined in political terms and in not having developed an ensemble of professional actors. This study of only seven contemporary directors has shown how difficult it is for one person to reconcile all the different functions the director may be expected to fill in today's theatre; but it is in the way they combine these different functions that the great directors have acquired identifiable styles and have made it possible to speak of 'directors' theatre' at all. Wilson's productions bear the stamp of his particular style as unmistakably as Magritte's paintings do of his. Wilson has achieved this by treating production as primarily a visual art form – words are always secondary, although they may have a significant part to play, as in *Alcestis*. This does not make him a greater director than those, such as Planchon or Stein, who have given greater importance to the verbal text. But it makes him the supreme artist of moving images working in the theatre today and the legitimate heir of those earlier directors, such as Edward Gordon Craig and Artaud, who looked forward to a time when the director would become the controlling magus of the modern stage.

Notes

1. The Rise of the Director

1. Edward Braun, *The Director and the Stage* (London: Methuen, 1982) pp. 14, 11.

2. Roger Planchon, preface to *L'Avare* (Paris: Livre de Poche, 1986) p. 7.

3. Jonathan Miller, *Subsequent Performances* (London: Faber, 1986) p. 70.

4. André Antoine, 'Causerie sur le théâtre' (1903) repr. in *Directors on Directing*, ed. Toby Cole and Helen Crich Chinoy (New York: Bobbs-Merrill, 1963) pp. 94, 95, 100.

5. Cited in Lawson Carter, *Zola and the Theatre* (New Haven: Conn.: Yale University Press, 1963) p. 87.

6. Cited in Braun, *The Director and the Stage*, p. 60.

7. Peter Brook, *The Empty Space* (Harmondsworth: Penguin, 1968) pp. 113–4.

8. Edward Gordon Craig, *On the Art of the Theatre* (London: Heinemann, 1911) pp. 180–1.

9. See *Meyerhold on Theatre*, ed. and tr. Edward Braun (New York: Hill and Wang; and London: Methuen, 1969) p. 50.

10. Cited in *Directors on Directing*, p. 297.

11. 'The Street Scene', in *Brecht on Theatre*, ed. and tr. John Willett (New York: Hill and Wang, 1964) p. 125.

12. Carl Weber, 'Brecht as Director', *Drama Review*, T37 (Fall, 1967) 105.

262

Notes

13. Interview in *Theatre Quarterley*, v, no. 18 (1975) 12.

2. Joan Littlewood

1. Ewan MacColl, 'Theatre of Action, Manchester', in Raphael Samuel, Ewan MacColl and Stuart Cosgrove, *Theatres of the Left 1880–1935* (London: Routledge and Kegan Paul, 1985) p. 230.
2. Howard Goorney, *The Theatre Workshop Story* (London: Methuen, 1981).
3. Ibid., p. 185.
4. *Agit-Prop to Theatre Workshop, Political Playscripts 1930–50*, ed. Howard Goorney and Ewan MacColl (Manchester: Manchester University Press, 1986) p. 36.
5. Cited in Goorney, *The Theatre Workshop Story*, pp. 41–2.
6. Ibid., pp. 166–167.
7. Ibid., p. 45.
8. See note 4.
9. Cited in Michael Coren, *Theatre Royal: 100 Years of Stratford East* (London: Quartet, 1984) p. 30.
10. Cited in Goorney, *The Theatre Workshop Story*, p. 154.
11. Ibid., p. 185.
12. Cited in Sean McCarthy and Hilary Norris, 'Revenons à nos moutons', *Theatrephile*, I, 4 (1984) 61.
13. Cited in Coren, *Theatre Royal*, p. 46.
14. Cited in Goorney, *The Theatre Workshop Story*, pp. 183–4.

3. Roger Planchon

1. Michael Kustow, 'Life and Work of an Illuminated Man', *Theatre Quarterly*, II, no. 5 (1972) 43.
2. Interview in *Etudes*, Aug 1977, p. 220.
3. Discussion with Arthur Adamov and René Allio in Arthur Adamov, *Ici et Maintenant* (Paris: Gallimard, 1964) p. 214.
4. André Gisselbrecht, '*Henry IV* de William Shakespeare', repr. in *Itinéraire de Planchon* (Paris: L'Arche, 1970) pp. 43–54.
5. Michel Bataillon, *Expoplanchon* [catalogue of exhibition] (Vénissieux: Centre Culturel Boris Vian, 1982).
6. Bernard Dort, '*Schweyk dans la deuxième guerre mondiale*', repr. in *Itinéraire de Planchon*, p. 83.
7. Planchon, 'Orthodoxies', *Théâtre populaire*, 46 (1962) 134.
8. Denis Bablet, 'Deux Schweyk', ibid., p. 108.
9. Interview in *Etudes*, Aug 1977, p. 228.
10. Interview in *Théâtre en Europe*, 9 (1986) 80.

Directors' Theatre

11. Interview in *Le Nouvel observateur*, 17 Nov 1980.

12. For a thorough discussion of Planchon's own plays and their staging, see Yvette Daoust, *Roger Planchon, Director and Playwright* (Cambridge: University Press, 1981); also David Bradby, *The Theatre of Roger Planchon* [slide set] (Cambridge: Chadwyck-Healey, 1984).

13. Interview in *Etudes*, Aug 1977, p. 234.

4. Ariane Mnouchkine

1. Marie-Louise and Denis Bablet, *Le Théâtre du Soleil* (Paris: CNRS, 1979) p. 7.

2. Interview in *Travail théâtral*, 2 (1971) 15–17.

3. *L'Age d'or* (Paris: Stock, 1975) p. 19.

4. Interview in *Theatre Quarterly*, v, no. 18 (1975) 10.

5. For a fuller account of Mnouchkine's productions in the 1970s and of the film about Molière, see David Bradby, *Modern French Drama 1940–80* (Cambridge: Cambridge University Press, 1984).

6. Interview in *Théâtre public*, 46–7 (1982) 8–11.

7. Interview in *Théâtre en Europe*, 3 (1984) 91.

8. Gilles Sandier, in *Le Matin*, 19 Dec 81.

9. *Acteurs*, Oct 1985.

10. Interview in *Théâtre en Europe*, 3 (1984) 91.

11. Ibid., p. 84.

5. Jerzy Grotowski

1. Throughout this chapter we are indebted to Jennifer Kumiega's *The Theatre of Grotowski* (London: Methuen, 1985), a thorough work of scholarship providing the most detailed analysis available in English of the sum of Grotowski's work to date.

2. Cited in Eugenio Barba, 'Theatre Laboratory 13 Rzedow', *Drama Review*, T27 (Spring 1965) 157.

3. Michael Kustow, 'Ludens Mysterium Tremendum et Fascinosum', *Encore*, Oct 1963, p. 14.

4. Grotowski, *Towards a Poor Theatre* (London: Eyre Methuen, 1975) p. 25.

5. Ibid., p. 16. Cf. Peter Brook's avowed aim in *The Empty Space* (Harmondsworth: Penguin, 1968) to 'bring the actor again and again to his own barriers, to the points where, in the place of new-found truth he normally substitutes a lie. . . . If the actor can find and see this moment he can perhaps open himself to a deeper, more creative impulse' (p. 126).

6. Grotowski, *Towards a Poor Theatre*, p. 16.

264

Notes

7. 'Conversations with Ludwik Flaszen', *Educational Theatre Journal*, 30, no. 3 (1978) 311.

8. Grotowski, *Towards a Poor Theatre*, p. 47. To describe this process, Grotowski prefers the terms 'study' or 'sketch' to 'improvisation', which he feels to have been denuded of meaning by an American *avant-garde* which had misunderstood the links to personal consciousness and structuring.

9. See Kumiega, *The Theatre of Grotowski*, pp. 239–71, for a detailed 'personal account' of *Apocalypsis* in performance, including translations of all textual material used.

10. 'Conversations with Ludwik Flaszen', *Educational Theatre Journal*, 30, no. 3 (1978) pp. 323–4.

11. Grotowski, *Towards a Poor Theatre*, p. 40.

12. Ibid., p. 98.

13. 'Holiday – the Day that is Holy', tr. from Grotowski's Polish original by Boleslaw Taborski, *Drama Review*, T58 (June 1973) 116. The Polish word for 'holiday' (*swięto*) is used to designate religious and secular holidays; etymologically it is attached to the word for light. For Grotowski it signifies a holy day, a privileged, inspirational time and space for purity and celebration.

14. Ibid.

15. Ibid.

6. Peter Brook

1. Brook in Penelope Houston and Tom Milne, 'Interview with Peter Brook', *Sight and Sound*, 32, no. 3 (Summer 1963) 109.

2. Brook in *A Midsummer Night's Dream*, Royal Shakespeare Company acting edition (Chicago: Dramatic Publishing Co., 1974) p. 30.

3. Brook, *The Empty Space* (Penguin, 1968) pp. 108–9.

4. Sally Jacobs in *A Midsummer Night's Dream*, p. 48.

5. John Kane, *The Sunday Times*, 13 June 1971.

6. Ibid.

7. Brook, in Michael Gibson, 'Brook's Africa', *Drama Review*, T59 (Sep 1973) 46–7.

8. Brook, in A. C. H. Smith, *'Orghast' at Persepolis* (London: Eyre Methuen, 1972) p. 249.

9. Brook, 'The Complete Truth is Global', *New York Times*, 20 Jan 1974.

10. Brook, 'The Three Cultures of Modern Man', *Cultures* (UNESCO Press and La Baconnière, Paris), 3, no. 4 (1976).

11. Ted Hughes in Smith, *'Orghast' at Persepolis*, p. 45.

12. Richard Peaslee, ibid., p. 120.

13. Brook, in Peter Wilson, 'Sessions in the USA: A Chronicle' (Paris: CIRT, 1973, unpublished) p. 25.

14. Antonin Artaud, *Collected Works*, IV (London: Calder and Boyars, 1974) 75.

15. Brook, *The Sunday Times*, 4 Jan 1976.

16. Brook, in Michael Billington, 'Written on the Wind: The Dramatic Art of Peter Brook', *The Listener*, 21/28 Dec 1978, p. 849.

17. Brook, *New York Times*, 4 May 1980.

7. Peter Stein

1. For a fuller account of this and other Stein productions, see Michael Patterson, *Peter Stein, Germany's Leading Theatre Director* (Cambridge: Cambridge University Press, 1981).

2. Interview in *Theater* (New Haven, Conn.) IX, no. 1 (Fall 1977) 50.

3. From Botho Strauss, *Tasso-Regiebuch*, cited in Patterson, *Peter Stein*, p. 23.

4. Interview in *Travail théâtral*, 9 (1972) 16–36.

5. Ibid.

6. Peter Iden, *Die Schaubühne am Halleschen Ufer 1970–9* (Frankfurt am Main: Fischer, 1982) p. 105.

7. 'The Irresistible Rise of the Schaubühne am Halleschen Ufer: A Retrospective of the West Berlin Theatre Collective', *Theater*, IX, no. 1 (Fall 1977) 23.

8. As note 4.

9. Interview in *Théâtre en Europe*, 1 (1984) 26.

10. Cited in Peter Lackner, 'Peter Stein', *Drama Review*, T74 (June 1977) 98.

11. Patterson, *Peter Stein*, pp. 144–5.

12. *Théâtre en Europe*, 1, p. 27.

8. Robert Wilson

1. These drawings and paintings, as well as the scenic objects designed by Wilson for use in performances, have been exhibited in museums and public galleries. They have become collectors' pieces, the money they create being fed back into the theatre performances.

2. Cf. John Cage in *Silence* (Cambridge, Mass: MIT Press, 1939) p. 93 – one of very few direct influences Wilson readily admits to: 'In Zen they say that if some thing is boring after 2 minutes, try it for 4. If still boring, try it for 8, 16, 32 and so on. Eventually one discovers that it is not boring at all, but very interesting.'

3. Louis Aragon, 'Lettre ouverte à André Breton sur le *Regard du*

Notes

sourd: l'art, la science et la liberté', repr. in *Eclats*, by Jean-Denis Bredin and Jack Lang (Paris: Jean-Claude Simoën, 1978). In English in *Performing Arts Journal*, I, no. 1 (1976).

4. The design bears an uncanny resemblance to the Swiss designer Adolphe Appia's 'rhythmic designs' for Dalcroze in 1909, created in response to the need for 'sets which established and emphasised their mass and volume unambiguously for the viewer, because only within the context of such an arrangement could the actor's body itself be seen to occupy and require space rhythmically – that is, to be engaged in active and living movement which could be perceived and measured in terms of the static objects around it. . . . Their rigidity, sharp lines and angles, and immobility, when confronted by the softness, subtlety and movement of the body, would, by opposition, take on a kind of borrowed life . . . a strong sense of rhythm' – *New Theatre Quarterly*, 1, no. 2 (1985) pp. 156–8.

5. In themselves, these sticks form part of a recurrent visual motif; they reappear as Hess' rake, Siegfried's sword in his cosmic battle with a dinosaur, the baton that an orchestral conductor employs to establish the rhythm of his delivery of a 'history of the earth'.

6. Asked what he regards as the function of mythology in contemporary theatre, Müller has said, 'The dead are in an overwhelming majority when compared with the living. And Europe has a wealth of dead stored up on that side of the ledger . . . you have to write for a majority. This is socialist realism.' And, echoing Wilson's aesthetic: 'the political task of art today is precisely the mobilisation of imagination'. Quoted in *Performing Arts Journal*, 10, no. 1 (1986) 96–7 and 105.

Index

Index

271

Index

Index

Index